BILBAO & SAN SEBASTIÁN

TOP EXPERIENCES • LOCAL LIFE

PAUL STAFFORD, ESME FOX

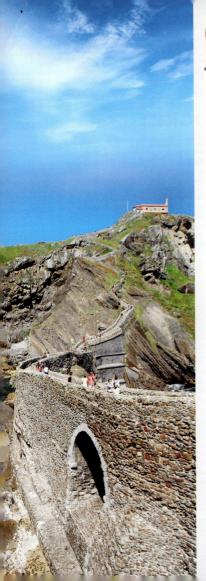

Contents

Plan Your Trip

Welcome To	4
Bilbao & San Sebastián's Top Experiences	6
Dining Out	12
Bar Open	16
Responsible Travel	20
Treasure Hunt	22
Museums & Public Art	23
Architecture	24
For Free	25
For Kids	26
Active Bilbao & San Sebastián	27
Beaches	28
Under the Radar Bilbao & San Sebastián	29
Four Perfect Days	30
Need to Know	32
Bilbao Neighbourhoods	34
San Sebastián Neighbourhoods	102

San Juan de Gaztelugatxe (p95)
ANASTASIA KAMYSHEVA/SHUTTERSTOCK ©

Explore Bilbao 35

Bilbao Old Town
(Casco Viejo) 37

Bilbao New Town.............. 53

Getxo & Portugalete.......... 75

Central Basque Coast...... 91

Explore San Sebastián 103

San Sebastián
Parte Vieja 105

San Sebastián New
Town & Monte Igueldo ... 123

San Sebastián Gros......... 141

Hondarribia & Pasaia 149

Worth a Trip

Understand the Past
at Gernika 88

Walking Tours

Bar-Hopping in Bilbao..... 38

Go on an Architecture
Tour of the New Town...... 60

Seaside Ramble in Getxo .. 76

Follow the Pintxo Trail..... 110

Old & New in
San Sebastián 128

Survival Guide 159

Before You Go 160

Arriving in Bilbao &
San Sebastián 161

Getting Around 162

Essential Information 163

Language 168

Index 171

Special Features

Museo Guggenheim
Bilbao 54

Watch Athletic Bilbao
on their Home Ground 58

Getaria 92

San Telmo Museoa 106

Aquarium 108

Playa de la Concha 124

Monte Igueldo 126

St-Jean de Luz,
France.............................. 156

Welcome to Bilbao & San Sebastián

Backed by the Basque Country's vineyard-ribboned hills, forests and orchards, postindustrial Bilbao, a cultural powerhouse with iconic architecture and art, and seaside San Sebastián, famed for its belle époque promenades and pumping surf, are linked by a string of picturesque coastal villages. The region's renowned culinary scene spans from creative bite-sized *pintxos* (Basque tapas) to multi Michelin-starred gastronomy.

San Sebastián

Bilbao & San Sebastián's Top Experiences

Explore the iconic Museo Guggenheim Bilbao (p54)

Watch Athletic Bilbao on their home ground (p58)

Understand the past at Gernika (p88)

Discover coastal Basque lifestyle in Getaria (p92)

Delve into Basque Culture and Society at San Telmo Museoa (p106)

Enter an aquatic wonderland at Aquarium (p108)

Hit the beach at Playa de la Concha (p124)

Enjoy mountaintop views at Monte Igueldo (p126)

Dining Out

The Basque Country is famous the world over for its cuisine. Whether you're stopping for a glass of wine and a few bite-sized pintxos at a local bar in Bilbao, San Sebastián or a coastal village, or savouring cutting-edge gastronomy at a Michelin-starred restaurant, you're bound to have a memorable food experience.

Pintxos

Enter any bar in the region and the counter is sure to be groaning under the weight of a small mountain of tiny plates of culinary art. These are *pintxos* (Basque tapas), which will redefine your interpretation of the bar snack. The best are often the hot ones made to order.

Basque Cuisine

The Basque Coast gives rise to superb seafood dishes, such as *bacalao al pil-pil* (salted cod and garlic in an olive-oil emulsion) and *chipirones en su tinta* (baby squid in its own ink), while the lush hills and mountains are the source of *chuleton de buey* (steaks – invariably massive).

Best Pintxos

La Cuchara de San Telmo Arguably one of the best *pintxo* bars in San Sebastián. (p111)

Antonio Bar The pick of the *pintxo* bars in San Sebastián's New Town. (p133)

La Viña del Ensanche Go for the tasting menu at Bilbao's standout *pintxo* bar. (p65)

Best Basque

Casa Victor Montes Bilbao landmark with exquisite *pintxos* and prized steaks (pictured, p42).

Gastroteka Danontzat A fun, creative spot in the cobblestone centre of Hondarribia. (p152)

Tamarises Izarra Contemporary Basque cuisine in Getxo. (p82)

Bascook High-end culinary wizardry set in an atmospheric former Bilbao salt warehouse. (p67)

Bodegón Alejandro Elegant cellar restaurant in San Sebastián. (p116)

La Txuleteria This traditional spot in San Sebastián's Gros gets the basics of Basque cuisine spot-on. (p145)

Casa Urola San Sebastián stalwart with hams hanging overhead. (p116)

M RAMÍREZ/ALAMY STOCK PHOTO ©

Best Seafood

Mesón Arropain Magnificent fish plates and seafood appetisers at this elegant spot in Lekeitio. (p98)

Casa Cámara Set out over the water in Pasaia, with a live-seafood cage lowered through the floor. (p153)

El Puertito Slurp down oysters and sip crisp white wine at this garrulous den near Bilbao's stadium. (p67)

Amelia Seafood tasting menus worthy of two Michelin stars beside Playa de la Concha. (p134)

Karola Etxea Dine on fresh seafood in a former fishing village above Getxo's Puerto Viejo. (p82)

Best International

Basquery Contemporary flavours in Bilbao's new town pair with the in-house brews. (p69)

Gerald's Bar San Sebastián outpost of a Melbourne restaurant with an international palate. (p144)

Seeing Stars

With 33 Michelin stars and two Michelin green stars, the Basque Country is a gourmet's nirvana. The following once-in-a-lifetime-experiences hog many of the 16 stars found in and around San Sebastián.

Arzak (www.arzak.es) Three stars; 3.5km east of San Sebastián.

Akelaŕe (www.akelarre.net) Three stars; 7km west of San Sebastián.

Martín Berasategui (www.martinberasategui.com) Three stars; 9km southwest of San Sebastián.

Bilbao & San Sebastián on a Plate
Pintxos

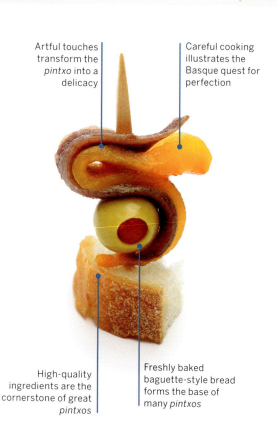

Artful touches transform the *pintxo* into a delicacy

Careful cooking illustrates the Basque quest for perfection

High-quality ingredients are the cornerstone of great *pintxos*

Freshly baked baguette-style bread forms the base of many *pintxos*

★ Top Five for Pintxos

La Viña del Ensanche (p65) A Bilbao classic since 1927.

Gure Toki (p43) Top choice on Bilbao's Plaza Nueva.

Bar Sport (p111) Misleading name, uniquely Basque bites in San Sebastián.

La Cuchara de San Telmo (p111) One of San Sebastián's best *pintxo* bars.

Casa Valles (p135) Home of the *gilda* (olive, anchovy and pickled pepper), the original *pintxo*, in San Sebastián.

Pintxos in the Basque Country

A showcase for the Basque Country's bountiful produce, *pintxos* come in limitless varieties, incorporating grilled prawns, plump anchovies, cod, tender squid, spider crab, juicy stuffed peppers, wild mushrooms, Idiazabal cheese, air-dried ham, earthy *morcilla* (blood sausage) and much more. Wherever you go, expect deliciously inventive fare, as creativity is a hallmark of these Basque delicacies.

Gure Toki (p43)

Bar Open

While the Basque Country may not be famous for its nightlife, there's a lot happening if you know where to look. You'll find a mix of buzzing cafes, convivial wine bars and lovely shaded terraces. Later on, you can join the party-minded crowds at bars, nightclubs and live music joints, with the revelry continuing late into the night.

Live Music & Culture

San Sebastián and Bilbao have an array of impressive venues that play a central role in their cultural life. Jazz, classical music, dance performances, live theatre, film screenings and opera are all part of the mix. The vibe is generally friendly and easy-going with a welcome lack of pretension. Venues' websites have details of upcoming gigs and performances.

Best Bars

Mala Gissona Beer House A lively local spot that serves the best craft brews in Gros. (p146)

La Gintonería Donostiarra Gin fans raise a glass at this G&T-loving Gros joint. (p146)

Ondarra The best place to head after a day on Playa de la Zurriola. (p146)

Pokhara One of the top places to start the night (or early afternoon) in San Sebastián's new town. (p136)

El Balcón de la Lola Bilbao's go-to late-night spot with a dance floor that draws in the party people. (p69)

Residence Catch live music or just stop in for a drink with a laid-back Bilbao crowd. (p69)

Best Old-School Spots

Museo del Whisky San Sebastián bar with a museum's worth of whisky and whisky paraphernalia. (p136)

Côte Bar An easy-going drinking den in San Sebastián's old town. (p118)

Bataplan Disco Get your groove on at this classic DJ-fuelled spot near Playa de la Concha. (p135)

Best Cafes

Alabama Café Welcoming cafe in Gros serving healthy food and some of the best coffee in town. (p145)

MIQUELITO/SHUTTERSTOCK ©

Koh Tao Slow down over a coffee or cool drink at this friendly San Sebastián cafe. (p137)

Baobab Riverside Bilbao cafe with regular jam sessions, poetry readings and an art-centric vibe. (p69)

Charamel Quirky cafe filled with eclectic decor in Bilbao's Casco Viejo. (p49)

Best Performing Arts

Kursaal San Sebastián's architecturally striking performing arts venue stages an impressive cultural line-up. (p146)

Teatro Victoria Eugenia Dating from 1912, this is a lavish San Sebastián theatre to catch a performance. (p138)

Tabakalera Celebrated San Sebastián cultural centre with film screenings and concerts. (p146)

Teatro Arriaga Take in a classical music concert in the neobaroque surrounds of Bilbao's beautiful old town theatre(pictured, p49).

Euskalduna Palace Enjoy classical music from Bilbao's two orchestras in this striking building. (p70)

Best Live Music

Kafe Antzokia The vibrant heart of Bilbao's contemporary Basque culture: music, public discussions (in Basque), a cafe and bar. (p70)

Altxerri Jazz Bar A San Sebastián temple to jazz and blues, hosting local and international musicians. (p120)

Le Bukowski One of San Sebastián's best places to hear eclectic bands from soul to rock. (p147)

Etxekalte Live jazz, experimental sounds and DJs near the waterfront in San Sebastián. (p120)

Bilborock Bilbao's concert venue for rock and metal lovers occupies an imaginatively converted 17th-century church. (p71)

Bilbao & San Sebastián in a Glass
Txakoli

Dry, lightly sparkling white wine

Poured from a height for a maximum bubble-to-drink ratio and flavour

Has a low alcohol content (typically 9% to 11%)

Drunk young as it doesn't keep longer than a year

Txakoli in the Basque Country

An aperitif that pairs perfectly with *pintxos*, *txakoli* (tcha-koh-*lee*) comes from three renowned districts. The most highly regarded is grown near Getaria, with vines covering the southeast-facing slopes just inland of the town. This wine has a very pale yellow to greenish colour. The other *txakoli*-producing regions are Bizkaia (Biscay Province), around Bilbao, and Álava, to Bilbao's south.

★ Top Five for Txakoli

Cork (p68) Bilbao wine bar run by a former Basque sommelier champion.

Vinoteka Ardoka (p155) Contemporary Hondarribia wine bar.

Rojo y Negro (p135) *Pintxo* bar in San Sebastián serving a *txakoli* sangria.

Lukas Gourmet Shop (p135) Shop a vast selection of *txakoli* and other Spanish wines in San Sebastián.

La Oka (p72) Pick up bottles to take home at this Bilbao gourmet shop.

Grapes used to make *txakoli*

Responsible Travel

Follow these tips when you're in Bilbao and San Sebastián to leave a lighter footprint, support local and have a positive impact on local communities.

Choose Sustainable Venues

Support sustainable sport Bilbao's Estadio San Mamés (www.athletic-club.eus) was among the first stadiums in Europe to be awarded a LEED (Leadership in Energy and Environmental Design) certification for its reduced environmental impact.

Have an eco-friendly night Increasingly, hotels are updating their environmental policies (eg reducing water usage and packaging) and obtaining official sustainability certifications (look out for the EU Ecolabel) to help you choose a reduced-impact stay.

Conscientious Dining

Shop for local ingredients A preference for fresh, local produce is one reason why Basque Country cuisine is so revered. Source your own ingredients from Erribera merkatua (Bilbao) or Mercado San Martín (San Sebastián; www.mercadosanmartin.es) and have a picnic beside the water.

Seek fine dining with green credentials At the verifiably world-class end of the scale, Michelin's green stars reward restaurants with pioneering sustainable practices. The Basque Country's two green stars are both found in the small town of Larrabetzu (13km east of Bilbao), at Eneko (https://eneko.restaurant) and Azurmendi (https://azurmendi.restaurant), which also has three regular stars.

Support Local

Embrace Basque culture While Spanish is universally spoken in the region, learning a few words of Euskara (the Basque language) is a sure-fire way to ingratiate yourself with locals. A good place to start is *kaixo* (hello, pron: kai-sho), *agur* (bye), *mesedez* (please) and *eskerrik asko* (thanks).

Explore the talents of local artisans and businesses Like all cities, Bilbao and San Sebastián are no strangers to a chain store, but independent stores thrive across the region too. San Sebastián's New Town and Bilbao's Casco Viejo are

UNAI HUIZI PHOTOGRAPHY/SHUTTERSTOCK ©

packed with stores selling local fashions, gourmet food, perfumes and musical instruments.

Leave a Small Footprint

Create your own footprints The Camino Norte, which forms part of the longer Camino de Santiago, strings together most of the seaside destinations in this book, as well as San Sebastián and Bilbao. Exploring the coastline on foot is a great way to really slow things down and discover local experiences that you won't find in the towns and cities.

Explore on two wheels or two feet The two cities are compact and pedestrian-friendly. Both also have shared-bike schemes with dozens of stations: Bilbaobizi (bilbaobizi.bilbao.eus/en/bilbao) in Bilbao and Dbizi (dbizi.eus) in San Sebastián. Both cities have extensive and ubiquitous networks of dedicated cycle lanes. If the weather is inclement, public transport is clean, reliable and regular.

Climate Change & Travel

It's impossible to ignore the impact we have when travelling, and the importance of making changes where we can.

Lonely Planet urges all travellers to engage with their travel carbon footprint. There are many carbon calculators online that allow travellers to estimate the carbon emissions generated by their journey; try resurgence.org/resources/carbon-calculator.html. Many airlines and booking sites offer travellers the option of offsetting the impact of greenhouse gas emissions by contributing to climate-friendly initiatives around the world.

We continue to offset the carbon footprint of all Lonely Planet staff travel, while recognising this is a mitigation more than a solution.

Treasure Hunt

NAEBLYS/SHUTTERSTOCK ©

The Basque Country has an enticing array of regional wares, locally made fashions and gourmet shops. The best places for indie stores and foodie spots are in the historic neighbourhoods of Bilbao (Casco Viejo) and San Sebastián (Parte Vieja). Elsewhere, you'll find a wide mix of small boutiques and brand-name favourites.

Best Basque Gifts & Souvenirs

Perfumería Benegas Sample perfumes including its house creations inside this long-running San Sebastián perfumery. (p138)

Alboka Artesanía One-of-a-kind Basque handicrafts from a little shop on San Sebastián's Plaza de la Constitución. (p121)

DendAZ All-Basque designers showcase their works in Bilbao. (p71)

Best Food & Drink

Lukas Gourmet Shop One of the best places in San Sebastián to pick up high-quality food and wine. (p135)

Mercado San Martín San Sebastián market dating back to 1884 and packed with culinary treasures. (p139)

Aitor Lasa Small but well-stocked San Sebastián food shop with all the essentials for a memorable picnic. (p121)

Mercado de la Ribera One of Spain's largest covered markets, this is where Bilbao's top chefs buy their ingredients (pictured, p50).

La Quesaría Aromatic little cheese (and wine) shop in Bilbao's old town. (p50)

La Oka Bilbao gourmet shop with wines, olive oils, sweets and other edibles by small Basque Country producers. (p72)

Almacen Coloniales y Bacalao Gregorio Martín For 80 years this Bilbao boutique has been selling only the finest *bacalao* (salted cod). (p51)

Best Fashion & Accessories

Ätakontu Graphic T-shirts by Bilbao textile artists. (p50)

Gorostiaga *Txapelas* (Basque berets) in Bilbao. (p50)

Peletería Ramón Ezkerra Leather handcrafted into trend-setting fashions in Bilbao. (p50)

Pukas Browse the latest beachwear at this San Sebastián surf specialist. (p143)

Loreak Mendian This Basque label has an excellent variety of men's and women's apparel in San Sebastián. (p139)

Museums & Public Art

MIKEDOTTA/SHUTTERSTOCK ©

Aside from the famed Museo Guggenheim Bilbao, the Basque Country is home to an outstanding collection of cultural treasures. You can also learn about the Basque people, their language and ancient traditions at regional museums covering history, archaeology and maritime lore.

Best for Art

Museo Guggenheim Bilbao Landmark museum flanked by iconic sculptures. (p54)

Azkuna Zentroa Contemporary art and modern design in an old wine storage facility in Bilbao. (p64)

San Telmo Museoa San Sebastián's overview of Basque culture through the ages, including impressive contemporary and classical art. (p106)

Construcción Vacía The brooding *Empty Space* sculpture sits below San Sebastián's Monte Urgull. (p144)

Statue of Christ Monte Urgull in San Sebastián is topped by a monumental statue of Christ that's dramatically floodlit at night. (p113)

Best for Basque History & Culture

Albaola Foundation A charming maritime museum in a working boatyard. (p153)

Arkeologi Museo Museum revealing how long Basques have lived here. (p42)

Museo de la Paz de Gernika An often heart-wrenching but thought-provoking museum of war and peace. (p89)

Cristóbal Balenciaga Museoa Browse exquisite pieces designed by Basque designer Cristóbal Balenciaga in his hometown, Getaria. (p93)

Captivating Creations

Chillida Leku's (www.museochillidaleku.com) rolling hills, 6km south of San Seabstián's Parte Vieja, are dotted with the captivating creations of revered local sculptor Eduardo Chillida, who also designed the site as a utopia where forest and sculptures harmonise. There are many additional works by Joan Miró here. The BU05 bus runs from New Town to the museum gate.

Architecture

Welcome to one of Europe's architecturally daring corners. Here you'll find the grand, the modern and the genre-changing. While a walk around any Basque city will reveal a cauldron of architectural styles, it's Bilbao that leads the way with bold works by Frank Gehry, Santiago Calatrava and Philippe Starck among others.

Best Contemporary Buildings

Museo Guggenheim Bilbao Visit throughout the day to admire the play of light on the titanium shell. (p54)

Azkuna Zentroa Multitasking Philippe Starck creation with cinemas, a rooftop swimming pool, cafes and restaurants in Bilbao. (p64)

Kursaal San Sebastián's beloved modernist work, the Kursaal cultural centre represents two beached rocks. (p146)

Estadio San Mamés Bilbao's state-of-the-art football stadium is a city landmark. (p58)

Best Historic Buildings

San Telmo Museoa Partially housed in a 16th-century convent, this San Sebastián museum also incorporates a modern extension. (p106)

Ayuntamiento A casino in the 19th century, San Sebastián's town hall is still opulent today. (p129)

Universidad de Deusto This Bilbao landmark was designed by architect Francisco de Cubas in 1886 to house the Jesuit university. (p72)

Concordia Train Station Built in Bilbao in 1902, featuring a handsome art-nouveau facade of wrought iron and tiles. (p61)

Castillo de Carlos V Strategically positioned on the hilltop of Hondarribia's old town, this castle is now a hotel. (p152)

Hotel Maria Cristina San Sebastián's most palatial hotel defines belle époque splendour. (p132)

Best Bridges

Puente Colgante The first-ever transporter bridge is a remarkable feat of engineering and a Unesco World Heritage Site in Portugalete. (p80)

Zubizuri The dazzling 1997-built 'White Bridge' by Santiago Calatrava helped transform Bilbao's cityscape (pictured, p64).

Puente de Maria Cristina Walk under the watchful eyes of angels on this belle époque bridge in San Sebastián. (p133)

For Free

SAIKO3P/SHUTTERSTOCK ©

One of the delights of Bilbao, San Sebastián and the Basque Country is that many of the more enjoyable sights and activities won't break the bank. In fact, they're often completely free, as are all of the region's beaches, markets, walking trails and plethora of picnic spots.

Best Free Cultural Sights

Koldo Mitxelena Kulturunea This free cultural centre in San Sebastián hosts innovative exhibitions. (p132)

Casa de la Historia Atop Monte Urgull in San Sebastián, this small museum provides an intriguing glimpse into Basque history. (p114)

Best Free Outdoor Experiences

Parque de Doña Casilda de Iturrizar The most beautiful park in Bilbao is whimsical, flowery and completely free. (p65)

Monte Urgull Wander the woodland paths to the top of Monte Urgull and enjoy stellar views over San Sebastián (pictured, p113.)

Parque de Cristina Enea San Sebastián's prettiest green space makes an enticing setting for a stroll. (p143)

Playa de la Concha Spending a day on San Sebastián's most famous beach doesn't cost anything (ice cream aside). (p124)

Las Siete Calles One of the most pleasant ways of exploring is strolling streets such as Bilbao's seven atmospheric lanes. (p41)

Isla de San Nicolás During low tide, it's good fun to walk out to this tiny island overlooking Lekeitio. (p98)

How to Save Money

○ Many museums and galleries in the region offer free entry one day a week.

○ The region's multitude of festivals (p48) are often free.

○ Students and seniors should bring ID and flash it at every opportunity for reduced prices.

For Kids

ALVARO GERMAN VILELA/SHUTTERSTOCK ©

Hands-on museums, boat and funicular rides, and lovely beaches and parks set the stage for a memorable family holiday in the family-friendly Basque Country, which has activities galore to inspire and amuse travellers of all ages.

Itsasmuseum Seafaring adventures await in Bilbao's stimulating maritime museum. (p64)

Aquarium Smile at the sharks and pet the blennies in San Sebastián's underwater world. (p108)

Funicular de Artxanda Bilbao's clanky funicular railway is a hit with children of all ages. (p65)

Isla de Santa Clara Take a boat ride out to Isla de Santa Clara off San Sebastián. (p115)

Monte Igueldo Funfair rides, ice cream and a funicular railway keep kids happy in San Sebastián (pictured, p126).

Playa de Ondarreta Calm seas, volleyball nets and sandcastles on this San Sebastián beach. (p132)

Albaola Foundation See a 16th-century whaling ship being built in Pasaia. (p153)

Cuevas de Santimamiñe Delve into this cave system outside of Gernika. (p89)

Plaza del Solar Dance to Sunday concerts on the Portugalete waterfront. (p80)

Castillo de la Mota Play king of the castle amid the cannons and ramparts of Monte Urgull's summit, overlooking San Sebastián. (p113)

Parque de Alderdi Eder Ride the colourful old carousel and watch the funny street performers on San Sebastián's seafront. (p133)

Basque Coast Geopark Peer back in time a few million years on a walk or boat tour from Zumaia. (p100)

Helpful Hints for Families

- Most restaurants welcome kids, although children's menus, high chairs and changing facilities are rare.

- Reserve baby cots when booking your hotel as numbers are often limited.

- Nappies (diapers) and formula are available at *farmacias* (pharmacies).

Active Bilbao & San Sebastián

ALVARO GERMAN VILELA/SHUTTERSTOCK ©

A renowned destination for surfing, the Basque Country has reliable waves all year round. Other water sports, such as kayaking and SUP (stand-up paddleboarding) are also popular, as is hiking along the spectacular coastline and in the hilly hinterland.

Best Surf Schools

Pukas Surf Eskola Ride San Sebastián's superb surf with Pukas. (p143)

Mundaka Surf Shop Hit Mundaka's fabled waves with this surf school. (p96)

Moor Surf Eskola Zarautz surf school on the promenade overlooking the beach. (p101)

Best Aquatic Activities

Bilboats Get a unique glimpse of Bilbao's architectural splendours on a Ría del Nervión boat tour. (p64)

Bilbobentura Join an organised paddle or hire a kayak or SUP in Bilbao. (p64)

Darwin Rentals Take a kayaking or SUP trip from San Sebastián's Parte Vieja. (p115)

Best Walking

Basque Coast Geopark Trails of varying lengths let you explore the coast's extraordinary geology. (p100)

San Sebastián to Pasaia Hike the 7.7km coastal trail, part of the Camino del Norte, linking Gros with Pasaia. (p143)

Paseo de Punta Galea Coastal walking path around the Punta Galea headland north of Getxo. (p84)

Ermita de Guadalupe to Pasaia Hike a 14km stretch of the Camino del Norte and meet Camino de Santiago pilgrims along the way. (p152)

Surf's Up: Top Tips For Hitting the Waves

○ Surf webcams and forecasts are available at magicseaweed.com and surfline.com.

○ Average water temperatures range from 12°C in February/March to 22°C in August.

○ Surf schools typically cater for all levels of ability, and hire equipment including wetsuits.

Beaches

The Basque Country's spectacular coastline ranges from tiny, rocky coves hidden down bumpy tracks to world-famous urban strands. For real fun, take a slow drive along the coast allowing time to find your own favourite hidden patch of sand.

POLIKI/SHUTTERSTOCK ©

Playa de la Concha Among the world's most beautiful, San Sebastián's city beach graces countless postcards. (p124)

Playa de la Zurriola San Sebastián's surf beach par excellence. (p143)

Playa de Ondarreta Gorgeous sweep of San Sebastián sand (pictured, p132).

Lekeitio During low tide, you can stroll from the sands out to the Isla de San Nicolás. (p97)

Playa de Hondarribia Calm waters make this family-friendly beach a prime swimming spot for young kids. (p151)

Hendaye A quick ferry ride from Hondarribia, this French beauty has a lovely stretch of shoreline. (p155)

Playa de Ereaga Getxo's sheltered sandy strip is just a metro ride away from downtown Bilbao. (p82)

Playa de Arrigunaga This Getxo beach sees offshore surf and on-shore skater action. (p77)

Playa de Laida Paddle out from Mundaka to these golden sands and surf breaks beyond. (p96)

Zarautz This small coastal village backs onto the region's longest swath of sand. (p100)

Staying Safe

- Tides vary greatly in the Basque Country, and broad stretches of sand can quickly be swallowed up by the incoming waters.

- Most beaches are patrolled by lifeguards in July and August; at other times, check locally to ensure conditions are safe for swimming.

- Sunbathing topless is acceptable on all beaches; tourist offices can advise on beaches where nudist sunbathing is permitted.

Under the Radar Bilbao & San Sebastián

Bilbao and San Sebastián are renowned for big-hitting attractions like the Museo Guggenheim Bilbao and storied beaches such as San Sebastián's Playa de la Concha, but there's plenty to discover off the beaten track, whether you're exploring the cities, up in the forested hinterland or along the beautiful Basque coast.

JAVIER CLICK MARTINEZ/SHUTTERSTOCK ©

Explore Local Neighbourhoods

Until the COVID-19 pandemic impacted international travel, the Basque Country received some 3.4 million overnight visitors annually. Many descend on the narrow streets of the cities' old towns, Bilbao's Casco Viejo and San Sebastián's Parte Vieja. Venturing beyond them in Bilbao brings you to intriguing areas like medieval Portugalete and the municipality of Getxo, with sandy beaches, scenic waterfront paths and traditional seafood restaurants. While in the backstreets of San Sebastián's New Town and the cool, young seaside neighbourhood of Gros, you'll find great shops, eateries and lively local hangouts.

Best Sights & Activities

Parque de Cristina Enea Stroll the wooded paths and lawns of this locally loved San Sebastián park. (p143)

Chillida Leku Explore the sculpture-dotted landscape at this fascinating museum near San Sebastián.

Sagardoetxea Sample locally made apple cider and tour the orchards before experiencing the festive cider-hall atmosphere. (p137)

Arrantzaleen Museoa Understand the importance of Basque fishing over the centuries at Bermeo's maritime museum. (p95)

Best Seaside Experiences

Playa de Murgita Cool off mid-hike at this hidden beach located between San Sebastián and Pasaia. (p143)

Crusoe Treasure Head out to sea to sample wines from the world's first underwater winery, or try them on shore. (p96)

Playa de Ereaga Laze on a sunbed at this favourite in Gexto. (p82)

Playa de Izturun Spot ammonites and other fossils among cliffs at Zumaia's western beach.

Four Perfect Days

Day 1 – Bilbao

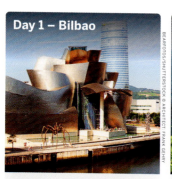

Stroll along Bilbao's river, stopping at Santiago Calatrava's eye-catching **Zubizuri** (p61). Continue to the **Museo Guggenheim Bilbao** (pictured, p50), allowing time to admire the exterior and surrounding sculptures. For lunch, feast on Basque delicacies at **La Viña del Ensanche** (p62).

Walk through dreamy **Parque de Doña Casilda de Iturrizar** (p61) and on to **Museo de Bellas Artes** (p54) for Bilbao's best collection of Basque and Spanish artists. Continue to **Euskal Museoa** (p37) for a Basque history lesson.

In the evening wander through the Casco Viejo, grazing on *pintxos* at **Casa Victor Montes** (pictured; p39) and enjoying drinks and live music at **Kafe Antzokia** (p68).

Day 2 – San Sebastián

Skip the motorway to San Sebastián, and instead take a slow, spectacular drive along the undulating coast road. Visit Portugalete's Unesco-listed **Puente Colgante** (p80), then head east to the jaw-dropping **San Juan de Gaztelugatxe** (pictured, p95).

For lunch, make your way to Lekeitio for a seafood feast at **Mesón Arropain** (p98), then take a siesta on the sublime beachfront. If the tide is low, walk out to the **Isla de San Nicolás** (p98).

Continue to seaside **Getaria** (p92), strolling its picturesque lanes before viewing the exquisite designs of the town's most famous son at the **Cristóbal Balenciaga Museoa** (p93). As the day cools, make for the world-renowned *pintxo* bars of San Sebastián.

Day 2 – San Sebastián

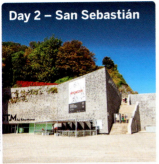

Start with a crash course in Basque culture at **San Telmo Museoa** (pictured, p106), check out the living exhibits in the city's stellar **Aquarium** (p108), then climb nearby **Monte Urgull** (p113) for magnificent city views.

For lunch, sample fried fish by the harbour or legendary *pintxos* in the old town. Afterwards, worship the sun on San Sebastián's near-perfect beaches: try **Playa de la Concha** (p124) for gentle waves or **Playa de la Zurriola** (p143) for surf.

In the early evening, explore Gros' indie boutiques, cafes and *pintxo* bars along Calle de Peña y Goñi.

End the night with a concert at the **Kursaal** (p146) or with drinks and live music at **Le Bukowski** (p147).

Day 4 – Hondarribia

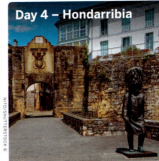

Today, head out of San Sebastián. Kick off in Pasaia, a short bus ride from town (or better yet a three-hour hike). Explore the area's whaling history at **Albaola Foundation** (p153) then cross the bay to the cobbled alleys and charming buildings of the Pasai Donibane side. Grab lunch at **Casa Cámara** (p153).

Push on to Hondarribia's photogenic walled centre, the **Casco Histórico** (pictured, p151). For a change of scene, check out the town's seafront promenade and, weather permitting, swim at the sheltered beach, the **Playa de Hondarribia** (p151).

Spend the evening on **Calle San Pedro** (p151), Hondarribia's prettiest, liveliest street. Buzzing *pintxo* bar **Gran Sol** (p154) is a great place to start.

Need to Know
For detailed information, see Survival Guide (p158)

Language
Spanish (Castilian) & Basque (Euskara).

Currency
Euro (€)

Visas
Not required for EU or Schengen country citizens. Other nationals need ETIAS pre-authorisation; some require a Schengen visa.

Money
ATMs widely available. Credit cards accepted in most hotels and restaurants.

Mobile Phones
Widely available local SIM cards can be used in compatible unlocked phones.

Time
Central European Time (GMT/UTC plus one hour)

Tipping
Not required, but rounding up is common.

Daily Budget

Budget: Less than €100
Dorm bed €15–30; *hostal* (budget hotel) and *pensión* (guesthouse) double €50–80
Multicourse *menú del día* lunch €11–15

Midrange: €100–200
Double room in midrange hotel €80–160
Lunch/dinner in decent restaurants €20–35

Top end: More than €200
Double room in top-end hotel from €160
Michelin-starred tasting menu from €90

Advance Planning

Three months before Book accommodation.
Two months before Book high-end restaurants.
One week before Book tours and concert tickets.

Useful Websites

Lonely Planet (www.lonelyplanet.com/spain) Information, bookings and traveller forum.

Basque Country (www.basquecountry-tourism.com) Regional authority.

San Sebastián Turismo (www.sansebastian-turismo.com) City authority.

Bilbao Turismo (www.bilbaoturismo.net) City authority.

Arriving in Bilbao & San Sebastián

Three airports serve this region: Bilbao, San Sebastián (domestic) and Biarritz, in France.

✈ From Bilbao Airport

Buses run every 15 to 30 minutes to central Bilbao (€3, 20 minutes), stopping at Plaza de Federico Moyúa and the Intermodal bus station. Taxis to the city centre cost €25 to €35. Buses to San Sebastián (€17.10, 1¼ hours, hourly) run directly from Bilbao's airport.

✈ From San Sebastián Airport

Buses E20 and E21 run hourly to San Sebastián (€2.65, 30 minutes). Taxis to the city centre cost €35 to €45.

✈ From Biarritz Airport

Buses link this airport in France with San Sebastián (€7, 45 minutes, up to eight daily).

Getting Around

M Bilbao Metro

Bilbao's two metro lines meet at Sarriko. The most useful stations are Moyúa, Abando and Casco Viejo. Trains run every few minutes from 6am until 11pm (to 2am Fridays, all night Saturdays).

🚋 Bilbao Tram

Bilbao's modern tram system runs from the Atxuri train station to La Casilla. Key stops include the Guggenheim, Teatro Arriaga and the Intermodal bus station.

🚌 Bus

Bilbobus runs Bilbao-wide bus services, although most places of visitor interest are within walking distance of one another. In compact San Sebastián, bus 16 from the city centre to Monte Igueldo is the most useful line for visitors.

Bilbao Neighbourhoods

Bilbao Old Town (Casco Viejo, p37)
A wanderer's delight, with attractive plazas, historic buildings and winding lanes. Come here for fabulous Basque food and historic architecture.

Bilbao New Town (p53)
Bilbao's new town has a diverse mix of architectural styles, food and shopping, world-class galleries and attention-grabbing sights

Museo Guggenheim Bilbao

Estadio San Mamés

Getxo & Portugalete (p75)
Just outside Bilbao and joined by the Unesco-listed Puente Colgante, Getxo and Portugalete have scenic waterfronts and excellent seafood restaurants.

Explore
Bilbao

Bilbao is infused with a seafaring history and proudly independent Basque spirit. In a glorious forest-fringed corner of northwestern Spain, it has an enchanting Old Town made up of narrow laneways and photogenic squares. It is also home to dramatic contemporary architecture and some fascinating museums.

Bilbao Old Town (Casco Viejo) **37**

Bilbao New Town **53**

Getxo & Portugalete **75**

Central Basque Coast **91**

Worth a Trip

Understand the Past at Gernika 88

Bilbao's Walking Tours

Bar-Hopping in Casco Viejo 38

Architecture Tour of the New Town 60

Seaside Ramble in Getxo 76

Following the Pintxo Trail 110

Explore

Bilbao Old Town (Casco Viejo)

The compact Casco Viejo, Bilbao's atmospheric old quarter, is full of charming streets, foodie shops, lively bars and fabulous cuisine. At the old town's heart are Bilbao's original seven streets, Las Siete Calles, which date from the 14th century.

The Short List

○ **Plaza Nueva (p39)** *Taking in the beauty of the old town's photogenic 19th-century square.*

○ **Arkeologi Museo (p42)** *Strolling through the ages amid Neolithic carvings, Roman statuary and Middle Ages finery.*

○ **Las Siete Calles (p41)** *Exploring the cobblestone lanes of Bilbao's oldest quarter.*

○ **Catedral de Santiago (p41)** *Checking out Bilbao's most important religious site, a Gothic Revival beauty dating back to the 1300s.*

○ **Teatro Arriaga (p49)** *Going for a tour or catching a show at this grand neobaroque theatre.*

Getting There & Around

M The Casco Viejo station is close to Plaza Nueva and the museums.

🚊 The Arriaga tram stop is near the Teatro Arriaga on the edge of the old town.

🚶 From the Museo Guggenheim, cross the river, turn right, and walk along the river to the Plaza del Arenal and the old town.

Bilbao Old Town Map on p40

Casco Viejo NORADOA/SHUTTERSTOCK ©

Walking Tour

Bar-Hopping in the Casco Viejo

One of the true highlights of a visit to Bilbao is the simple pleasure of sipping a glass of txakoli (local white wine) and nibbling on an artful pintxo (Basque tapa) in one of the city's many bars. This food- and drink-drenched route sees you hop from bar to bar, sampling wines and deliberating over which one serves the finest food.

Walk Facts

Start Plaza Nueva; M Casco Viejo

Finish Mercado de la Ribera; Ribera

Length 1km; two hours

❶ Plaza Nueva

Plaza Nueva (Plaza Barria) is awash with *pintxo* bars, children racing around and adults socialising over a drink and a tasty titbit. On Sunday mornings a flea market takes place – rummage through old records, books, postcards, crockery and all manner of assorted odds and ends.

❷ Sorgínzulo

Start off your foodie tour at **Sorgínzulo** (www.sorginzulo.com), a matchbox-sized place with an exemplary spread. The house special of fried calamari is only served on weekends; other standouts include *bacalao al pil-pil* (cod in a garlicky sauce).

❸ Café-Bar Bilbao

Continue your exploration of the square's culinary skills at the **Café-Bar Bilbao** (www.bilbao-cafebar.com), with its cool blue southern Spanish tiles, warm northern atmosphere and superb array of *pintxos*.

❹ Plaza Miguel Unamuno

Surrounded by many excellent *pintxos* bars, this busy plaza was named after Miguel de Unamuno (1864–1936), a famous writer, poet and philosopher who was born in Bilbao.

❺ Bar La Muga

Just off the plaza, lively **Bar La Muga** (www.lamuga.eus) serves an array of tasty *pintxos* in an industrial-style interior. Bites include mini burgers and quail egg and bacon, as well as several veggie options. Pair your *pintxo* with one of 11 beers on tap, including four artisanal.

❻ Plazuela de Santiago

At the heart of the Casco Viejo lies Plazuela de Santiago, where Siete Calles converge at the grand **Catedral de Santiago** (p41). Spend some time admiring this 14th-century masterpiece before continuing on for more tasty bites.

❼ Xukela

Sample a wide range of *pintxos* from the bar **Xukela** (www.facebook.com/xukela), set in a cosy tavern packed full of bookshelves, photographs and other odd knick-knacks.

❽ Mercado de la Ribera

Finish up at **Mercado de la Ribera** (p50), inaugurated in 1929. As well as food stalls, you'll find an array of excellent *pintxos* bars to keep you satisfied.

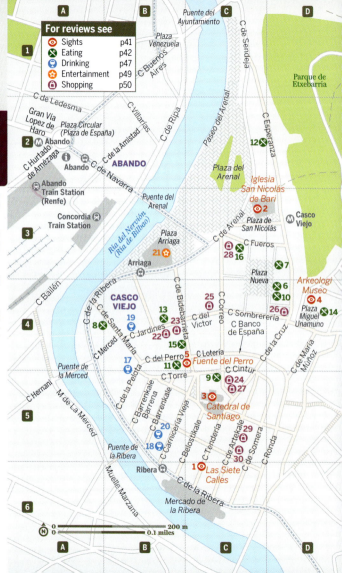

Sights

Las Siete Calles   AREA

1   MAP P40, C6

Forming the heart of Bilbao's Casco Viejo are seven streets known as the Siete Calles (Zazpi Kaleak in Basque).

These atmospheric lanes – Barrenkale Barrena, Barrenkale, Carnicería Vieja, Belostikale, Tendería, Artekale and Somera – date to the 1400s, when the east bank of the Ría del Nervión (Ría de Bilbao) was first developed.

They originally constituted the city's commercial centre and river port; these days they teem with lively cafes, *pintxo* bars and shops.

Iglesia San Nicolás de Bari   CHURCH

2   MAP P40, C3

This landmark church by the northern entrance to the Casco Viejo was consecrated in 1756. Dedicated to St Nicholas of Bari, the patron saint of sailors, it features a quadrangular baroque facade emblazoned with impressive heraldic stonework over the main portal, and two bell towers.

Catedral de Santiago   CATHEDRAL

3   MAP P40, C5

Towering above all in the Casco Viejo (although strangely invisible in the narrow streets) is the Catedral de Santiago, which has a vaulted cloister and Gothic Revival facade. Bilbao's oldest church,

Mercado de la Ribera (p50)

the cathedral dates back to the 14th century, though the Renaissance portico was added in 1571, following a fire. Above the main entrance, you'll spot scallop shells – symbols of Santiago (St James) and a reference for pilgrims on the northern route of the Camino de Santiago. (www.catedralbilbao.com)

Arkeologi Museo   MUSEUM

4 ⊙ MAP P40, D4

This two-storey museum takes you deep into the past, beginning with 430,000-year-old fossils found in the Sierra de Atapuerca. On the 2nd floor, as you romp through the ages, you'll see models of early fortified villages, Celtiberian carvings, and statues and fragments from the Roman period; descend into the Visigothic times and the ensuing Middle Ages. Stones for catapults, a 10th-century trephined skull and jewellery from the 1200s are other curiosities.

Fuente del Perro   FOUNTAIN

5 ⊙ MAP P40, C4

Designed by Juan Bautista de Oureta and Miguel de Maruri in 1800, this neoclassical fountain is located at a natural spring where market animals used to drink. Its three taps protrude from lion heads that more closely resemble their namesake *perro* (dog) heads. Spring water still flows here; bring a bottle to fill up.

Eating

Casa Victor Montes   BASQUE €€€

6 ✖ MAP P40, D4

The 1849-built Victor Montes attracts numerous luminaries but locals also appreciate its exquisite gilding, marble and frescoes, 1000-strong wine list and superb food.

Pintxos span foie gras with cider jelly to *lomo* (cured pork sausage)

Basque Language

The Basque language, known as Euskara, is the oldest in Europe and has no known connection to any Indo-European languages. Suppressed by Franco, Basque was subsequently recognised as one of Spain's official languages, with 751,500 speakers in total (a 6% growth rate in the past 25 years), of which 93% of speakers are on the Spanish side and 6.8% are on the French side (nearly all speakers are bilingual). It has become the language of choice among a growing number of young Basques in particular (51.5% of five- to 24-year-olds speak it).

While visiting, you'll find that speaking at least a few words of Basque is greatly appreciated by locals and will make your trip more rewarding. The one you'll hear the most is *agur*, which is used both as a greeting and to say goodbye.

History of the Lauburu

The most visible symbol of Basque culture is the lauburu, or Basque cross. 'Lauburu' means 'four heads' in Basque and it's so named because of the four comma-like heads. The meaning of this symbol is lost in the misty past – some say it represents the four old regions of the Basque Country, others that it represents spirit, life, consciousness and form – but today many regard it as a symbol of prosperity. It's also used to signify life and death, and so is found on old headstones. Another theory about its meaning is that it originally started appearing on 16th-century tombstones to indicate the grave of a healer of animals and souls (similar to a spiritual healer). When all is said and done, however, there's no real proof for any of these arguments.

with prawns and rum-soaked raisins. If you're planning a full meal, book in advance and savour the house special, *txuleta* (seven-year-old dairy cow T-bone steak for two; €63).

Past patrons include film director Oliver Stone, U2's Bono and architect Frank Gehry, who designed Bilbao's Museo Guggenheim here. (www.victormontes.com)

Gure Toki   PINTXOS €€

7 MAP P40, D3

One of the best *pintxo* bars in the Casco Viejo, this popular place serves creative and outstandingly good bites, including mini pastry parcels filled with stir-fried veg and prawns, *bacalao al pil-pil* and glass bowls filled with poached eggs, sauteed potatoes and mushrooms. (www.guretoki.com)

Irrintzi   PINTXOS €

8 MAP P40, A4

Located on Casco Viejo's western side, Irrintzi is a cosy, low-ceilinged eating and drinking spot, where a mostly local crowd files in for inventive bites not found elsewhere. Feast on tasty morsels such as falafels with shitake mushrooms, crab-and-lemon croquettes, and mini lamb kebabs. Lots of vegetarian options, plus gluten-free, if you ask at the bar. (www.irrintzi.es)

Baster   PINTXOS €€

9 MAP P40, C5

Chic Baster serves a range of outstanding *pintxos*, including octopus skewers with potato, mini quiches, house-made croquettes and delectable *jamón* (ham). Pair them with a glass of refreshing *txakoli* (local white wine) or vermouth, or choose from its extensive range of local craft beers.

It gets very busy at weekend lunchtimes, when bar-hoppers crowd its pavement tables and bright, modern interior. (www.facebook.com/BasterBilbao; 🛜)

Bar Charly

PINTXOS €

10 ❌ MAP P40, D4

In an unrivalled location on Plaza Nueva, Bar Charly lays out *pintxos* for garrulous afternoon and evening crowds. There are at least a couple of vegetarian *pintxos* per

The Art of Eating Pintxos

Just rolling the word *pintxo* ('pin-cho') around your tongue defines the essence of this cheerful, cheeky little slice of Basque cuisine. The perfect *pintxo* should have exquisite taste, texture and appearance, and should be savoured in just a few elegant bites. The Basque version of a *tapa*, the *pintxo* transcends the commonplace with its culinary panache.

Many *pintxos* are bedded on small pieces of bread or on tiny half-baguettes, upon which towering creations are constructed. Some bars specialise in seafood, with much use of marinated anchovies, prawns and strips of squid, all topped with anything from shredded crab to pâté. Others deal in pepper or mushroom delicacies, or simply offer a mix of everything. And the choice isn't normally limited to what's on the bar top in front of you: many of the best *pintxos* are the hot ones you need to order.

For many visitors, ordering *pintxos* can seem like one of the dark arts of local etiquette. Fear not: in many bars in Bilbao, San Sebastián and the Basque Country, it couldn't be easier. With so many *pintxo* varieties lined up along the bar, you can just ask for want you want. Otherwise, many places have a list of *pintxos*, either on a menu or posted up behind the bar. If you can't choose, ask for '*la especialidad de la casa*' (the house speciality) and it's hard to go wrong.

You can also order *raciones* (literally 'rations' or larger servings) or *medias raciones* (half-rations; bigger plates than tapas servings but smaller than standard *raciones*). These plates and half-plates of a particular dish are a good way to go if you particularly like something and want more than a mere *pintxo*. After a couple of *raciones*, however, most people are full.

Locals often prefer to just have one or two *pintxos* in each bar before moving on to the next place. Bear in mind that *pintxos* are never free. In fact, the cost of a few mouthfuls can quickly add up.

Casa Victor Montes (p42)

day, such as brie with jam and walnuts, or spinach and goat's-cheese croquettes; other dishes might include smoked salmon and anchovies with black caviar or crab mayonnaise. (www.facebook.com/barcharlybilbao; ✈)

Rio-Oja   BASQUE €€

11 ✖ MAP P40, B4

Going strong since 1959, Rio-Oja retains a rock-solid reputation for its traditional Basque dishes. Its *cazuelitas* (stews served in the clay ramekins in which they're cooked) are ideal for sharing – varieties include *cordero guisado* (braised lamb) and *chipirones en su tinta* (squid cooked in its own ink), as well as inland specialities such as snails, tripe and sheep brains.

Claudio: La Feria del Jamón   PINTXOS €

12 ✖ MAP P40, C2

A creaky old place full of ancient furnishings, Claudio has scarcely changed since it opened in 1948. As you'll guess from the name and the hams hanging from the ceiling, it's all about pigs, including *lomo* (air-dried pork loin), *morcilla* (blood sausage), chorizo and *salchichón* (smoked sausage), accompanied by local cheeses and wines. Opposite the bar is a shop selling hams. (www.claudiojamones.com)

Look Out for the Txikiteros

The *txikiteros* are groups of choral singers from Bilbao who get together before dinner and go from bar to bar (known as *poteo*) singing and drinking in the streets of the Casco Viejo.

They often dress in typical Basque clothes such as the traditional *txapelas* (Basque berets) and sing classic Basque songs called *bilbainadas*.

You can see them all year round, but particularly around 11 October on the day of the Virgin of Begoña, which has also become known as the day of the *txikiteros*.

In order to catch a glimpse of this tradition, hang around the bars in the old town, mostly around Plaza Nueva and the Siete Calles.

The most sacred spot for the *txikiteros*, however, is on the corner of Calle Pelota and Calle Santa María, where they'll take their leftover change to the Amatxu de Begoña (a religious building with the image of the Virgen de Begoña) to protect them for the future.

By Aitor Delgado, *Aitor is a tour guide at aitordelgado.com.*
@aitordelgadotours

Berton   PINTXOS €

13 MAP P40, B4

Tucked in a narrow lane, rustic Berton lures you in with a long wooden bar topped with tiny delicacies and frothy pilsner on tap. Glistening slices of *jamón*, deep-fried Gernika peppers, garlicky mushrooms, blood sausage with red pepper, and spider crab in squid ink are all served in an exposed-brick, stone and timber setting. (www.berton.eus; 📶)

Bacaicoa Taberna   BASQUE €

14 MAP P40, D4

This pint-sized bar tucked into the corner of Plaza Miguel Unamuno only offers four types of *pintxos*, but what they do, they do incredibly well. All the *pintxos* are made to order, so they come out of the kitchen piping hot and oh-so-fresh. Their speciality is mushrooms – think grilled garlicky *setas* (oyster-like mushrooms), juicy cremini mushrooms filled with spicy mayonnaise and wild mushroom croquetas.

They also do flame-grilled chorizo.

El Txoko Berria   BASQUE €€

15 MAP P40, B4

Set over two levels, with a beautifully tiled ground-floor dining room and a more contemporary space above, this welcoming restaurant excels at staples such as pork cheeks cooked in Rioja red wine, cod *bizkaina* style (with a sweet, slightly spicy pepper sauce) and risotto with mushrooms and Idiazabal sheep's cheese.

On weekdays, the three-course lunch menu (€12.50) is fantastic value. (www.eltxokoberria.com)

Los Fueros   BASQUE €€

16 MAP P40, C3

Seafood stars at this backstreet bar-restaurant near Plaza Nueva, appearing in dishes such as cider-marinated sardines, chargrilled octopus, mussels steamed in *txakoli* (white wine) and dorado with salsa verde. Extending to a mezzanine, the rustic-contemporary setting is more stylish than many old town places, decked out in off-white and jade-green mosaic tiling and gleaming timber tables. Reserve ahead. (www.losfueros.com)

Drinking

La Peña Athletic   BAR

17 MAP P40, B4

A must for all fans of Bilbao's famed football team, La Peña Athletic is covered with vintage jerseys, trophies, old team photos and oil paintings of legendary past players. It pulls a mix of old-timers and young enthusiasts, who come to raise a glass (and snack on *pintxos*) to the boys in red and white while watching a game. (www.restauranteathletic.com)

Pinxtos

Basque
Festivals & Events

The Basques love a good festival. Every town, city and most villages have their own week of mayhem, and during the summer you'll almost certainly come across a celebration on your travels. Highlights of the region's calendar include the following:

Aste Nagusia Held over nine days, Bilbao's grandest fiesta begins on the first Saturday after 15 August. Its full program of cultural events features music and dancing, Basque rural sports (such as chopping wood and lifting heavy stones), parades of giants and nightly fireworks.

Bay of Biscay Festival (www.bayofbiscayfestival.eus) In the Central Basque Coast town of Bermeo, this three-day festival (typically held in July) combines indie, rock and alternate concerts by Basque and Spanish bands with a celebration of the area's culinary scene, from Michelin-starred food trucks to cookery demonstrations and workshops.

Bilbao BBK Live (www.bilbaobbklive.com) Bilbao's biggest musical event draws top artists from around the globe. It takes place over three days (typically early to mid-July) in Parque Kobetamendi, a hillside park located 3km west of the centre.

Carnaval Both Bilbao and San Sebastián celebrate with parades over six days, from the Thursday before Ash Wednesday to Shrove Tuesday.

Getxo Jazz (www.getxo.eus) The line-up at Getxo's jazz festival (June or July) is usually impressive, featuring international stars on the main stage at Plaza Biotz Alai, along with free concerts by up-and-coming musicians on Plaza Estación de Algorta.

Dia de San Sebastián San Sebastián celebrates its patron saint with fervour (20 January). The big event is the Tamborrada, when thousands of drummers wearing 19th-century military dress and chefs' whites parade through the city.

San Sebastián International Film Festival (www.sansebastian festival.com) The world-renowned film festival (typically in September) usually features an excellent line-up of films from Europe, the US and Latin America, with a few big premieres. Screenings (around 200 to 250 in all) take place at venues citywide.

Semana Grande (http://astenagusia.donostiakultura.eus) Known as Aste Nagusia in Basque, San Sebastián's big summer festival features an action-packed line-up of street parties, concerts and nightly fireworks competitions, plus rural sports, children's activities, and parades with giants and oversized heads.

Bohemian Lane CAFE

18 MAP P40, B5

Inviting coffeehouse Bohemian Lane has wicker chairs, furniture made from salvaged wooden pallets and patterned cushions. A laid-back spot for fair trade coffee and tea, and organic fresh juices, it also has cakes, scones, croissants, cookies and other sweets that are 100% vegan. (www.bohemianlanebilbao.com)

Charamel CAFE

19 MAP P40, B4

This quirky cafe is filled with eclectic decor and serves some of the best coffee and pastries in the Casco Viejo. Relax on sink-down sofas or mismatched chairs and sink your teeth into rich cinnamon buns and flaky chocolate croissants.

Hells Bells BAR

20 MAP P40, B5

Plastered with posters, guitars and other memorabilia, dimly lit Hells Bells blasts out tracks from bands such as AC/DC, Judas Priest, Mötley Crüe, Kiss and Metallica, accompanied by cheap beer. If there's a rock or metal concert in Bilbao, you can be sure the after-party will be held here.

Entertainment

Teatro Arriaga THEATRE

21 MAP P40, B3

The neobaroque facade of this 1200-seat venue commands the open spaces of El Arenal between the Casco Viejo and the river. It stages theatrical performances

Teatro Arriaga

Mercado de la Ribera

Overlooking the river, the **Mercado de la Ribera** (Map p40, C6; www.mercadodelaribera.biz) is an expansive food market that draws many of the city's top chefs for their morning selection of fresh produce. If you're not planning a picnic, don't miss the *pintxo* counters upstairs (open till 10pm), which offer an excellent spread – plus seating indoors and out.

and classical music concerts. Guided behind-the-scenes tours lasting 50 minutes in English, Spanish and Basque (adult/child €5/free) take place hourly from 11am to 1pm on Saturdays and Sundays. (www.teatroarriaga.eus)

Shopping

Ätakontu

FASHION & ACCESSORIES

22 MAP P40, B4

A pair of Bilbao textile artists created this small shop, which is making waves across the Basque Country. Graphic T-shirts are the speciality, featuring whimsical and art-naïf designs (the dinosaur head is an icon); all are manufactured locally, made with organic cotton and come in unisex sizes.

And with limited production runs, you won't see these elsewhere. (www.atakontu.es)

La Quesaría

FOOD & DRINKS

23 MAP P40, B4

Cheese lovers shouldn't miss this wondrous shop. You'll find more than 40 varieties of the good stuff, with new selections every week. It's also worth browsing the selection of microbrews (try a pale ale from the Bidassoa Basque Brewery), wines, local jams and other goodies. (www.laqueseriabilbao.com)

Peletería Ramón Ezkerra

FASHION & ACCESSORIES

24 MAP P40, C5

At Bilbao-born Ramón Ezkerra's atelier, limited-edition pieces handcrafted from sustainably sourced Basque and Spanish leather are primarily made on site. Along with stylish jackets for men and women, you'll find bags, hats, gloves, leather dresses, jumpsuits and trousers. Clothing can be tailored to fit. (www.ramonezkerra.com)

Gorostiaga

HATS

25 MAP P40, C4

Gorostiaga has been crafting traditional *txapelas* (Basque berets) and hats since 1857. Its nine different berets cover all parts of the Basque Country, including the flat-topped berets worn in Bilbao, the tilted style of the French Basque Country, and the oversized *txapeldun* typically worn at festivals, weddings and other celebrations. (www.sombrerosgorostiaga.com)

Le Chocolat
CHOCOLATE

26 MAP P40, D4

The Bilbao-inspired treats here include chocolates in the shape of pavement tiles and Athletic Bilbao football boots.

At Christmas, it's also one of the best places for seasonal local speciality *sokonusko* – layered nougat based on a Mayan recipe brought back to the city by Bilbao adventurer Iñigo Urrutia, who travelled to Mexico in 1881 in search of El Dorado. (www.lechocolat.es)

Rzik
FASHION & ACCESSORIES

27 MAP P40, C5

Street fashion goes green at this hip little store, where everything is made from recycled materials.

You'll find colourful messenger bags made from old advertising banners, sleek backpacks made of truck tyres, eye-catching belts made from former firefighter hoses, and bicycle inner tubes reconfigured into wallets.

The designs are bright and bold – and make fine conversation pieces as well. (www.rzik.es)

Arrese
FOOD

28 MAP P40, C3

With almost two centuries of baking experience (it opened in 1836), you'd hope the cakes at this little patisserie would taste divine, and they do – even more than expected. Treats such as *pastel vasco* (almond cream torte), *goxua* (custard-topped sponge cake) and *tarta de Santiago* (almond tart from Galicia) are among its specialities. (www.arrese.biz)

Orriak
ARTS & CRAFTS

29 MAP P40, C5

Easy to miss, this delightful little shop is a great spot when browsing for gifts made in store or elsewhere in the Basque Country. Ceramic tiles, leaf cut-outs, wooden boxes and other crafts come emblazoned with Basque symbols. (www.orriak.com)

Almacen Coloniales y Bacalao Gregorio Martín
FOOD

30 MAP P40, C5

Specialising in *bacalao* (salted cod) from the Faroe Islands since 1931, this small store also sells oils, pulses and hams. (www.gregoriomartin.es)

Explore
Bilbao New Town

Bilbao's elegant new town has an impressive spread of attractions. The neighbourhood is home to world-class and fascinating architecture, museums, beautiful river views and walks, and some of the best restaurants and bars in the region.

The Short List

- **Museo Guggenheim Bilbao (p54)** *Exploring the iconic art and hidden facets of this astonishing architectural wonder.*

- **Museo de Bellas Artes (p70)** *Wandering through galleries lined with sculptures and paintings by renowned artists from the Basque Country and beyond.*

- **Estadio San Mamés (p58)** *Joining thousands of frenzied fans as they cheer on Athletic Bilbao.*

- **Azkuna Zentroa (p64)** *Checking out contemporary art and admiring the imaginative Alhóndiga cultural centre.*

- **Funicular de Artxanda (p65)** *Riding to the top of Artxanda for mesmerising city views.*

Getting There & Around

[M] Useful metro stations include Moyúa, bang in the heart of town; Abando for shopping, and San Mamés for the bus station and football stadium.

🚊 The tram runs along the length of the river with a stop close to the Museo Guggenheim Bilbao.

🚶 It's a 10-minute walk from the Museo Guggenheim Bilbao to the city centre.

Bilbao New Town Map on p62

Zubizuri Bridge (p64)
A G BAXTER/SHUTTERSTOCK © ARCHITECT: SANTIAGO CALATRAVA

Top Experience 📷
Explore the Iconic Museo Guggenheim Bilbao

 MAP P62, E1

www.guggenheim-bilbao.eus

Opened in 1997, Frank Ghery's titanic Museo Guggenheim Bilbao is the city's most striking building. The museum, filled with pieces from some of the world's best contemporary artists, was responsible for helping the city become the energetic creative hub it is today. For many travellers, this extraordinary building is the primary reason for visiting Bilbao.

The Design

For most visitors, it's the architecture itself that is the real star of the Guggenheim show. Designed by Canadian-born American architect Frank Gehry, the museum's flowing canopies, promontories, ship-like shapes, towers and flying fins, all covered in gleaming titanium tiles, are irresistible. Allow plenty of time to walk around the building's exterior, observing how the patterns and colours change with the light.

Puppy

Outside, on the city side of the museum, is Jeff Koons' kitsch *Puppy*, a 12m-tall Highland terrier made up of thousands of flowers. Originally a temporary exhibition, Bilbao has hung on to 'El Poop'. *Bilbaínos* will tell you that El Poop came first – and then they built a kennel behind it.

Tall Tree & the Eye

An exterior highlight is Anish Kapoor's work, *Tall Tree & the Eye*. It consists of 73 reflective spheres anchored around three axes, each of which distorts reality as you look into it.

Fog Sculpture #08025 (FOG)

Lying between the glass buttresses of the central atrium and Ría del Nervión (Ría de Bilbao) outside the museum is this installation by Fujiko Nakaya: a simple pool of water that regularly emits a mist. In case you missed the play on words here, FOG are also the initials of the building's architect.

Fire Fountain

Yves Klein's *Fire Fountain* was conceived by the artist but only realised here after his death. At night, its five jets of fire dance above a water-filled pool and illuminate the building's walls.

★ Top Tips

- Entry prices change throughout the year depending on the season and the exhibitions.
- Entry queues can be huge in busy times; you can prebook online for an allocated time slot.
- For a bird's-eye perspective of the museum, ride the Funicular de Artxanda (p65) to the park high above the city.

✕ Take a Break

The Guggenheim's Nerua (p67) restaurant serves refined Basque cuisine.

Less expensive is the excellent **Bistró Guggenheim Bilbao** (www.bistroguggenheimbilbao.com). Try the *torrija* (Basque French toast), it's the best in the city.

Maman

On the riverbank just outside the museum is Louise Bourgeois' sculpture *Maman*: (pictured p54) a skeletal, spider-like canopy said to symbolise a mother's protective embrace.

Atrium

The atrium, a huge cathedral-like space, serves as your first taste of the museum's interior. Light pours into this entrance gallery through what appear to be glass cliffs. At one end, Jenny Holzer's nine LED columns of ever-flowing phrases and text fragments (in English, Spanish and Basque) appear to reach for the skies. The space was designed to provide views of the river and surrounding hills.

Tulips

Another highlight to look out for is Jeff Koons' stainless steel *Tulips*, whose bubbly, colourful form in Christmas bauble–style high gloss represents a bouquet of giant balloon flowers (more than 2m tall and 5m across). The work belongs to his ambitious *Celebration* series.

The Matter of Time

The ground floor of the museum is devoted to permanent exhibitions. One of the most popular with visitors is Richard Serra's rust-red *The Matter of Time*. Despite the grand name, this is best described as a giant steel maze that visitors are free to wander through, which often seems to serve as much as a playground as a work of art.

Puppy by Jeff Koons (p55)

The Vision Behind the Masterpiece

Designed by celebrated architect Frank Gehry, the Museo Guggenheim Bilbao dominates the city's waterfront, its look and mood changing with the rising and falling light. The building sits on a former industrial wasteland and the city's shipping, industrial and fishing heritage is evoked in its form, which some describe as resembling a ship or a shimmering fish.

After the collapse of shipping and heavy industry in Bilbao, the authorities embarked on a regeneration of the city. One of the key requirements was a world-class cultural exhibition space, and from that idea came the Museo Guggenheim Bilbao.

Since its opening in 1997, the museum has done much to transform Bilbao from run-down industrial city to bonafide cultural hub. As well as playing off the city's historical and geographical context, the building reflects Gehry's own interests, not least his engagement with industrial materials. The titanium tiles that sheathe most of the building like giant scales are said to have been inspired by the architect's childhood fascination with fish.

In the room's northeastern corner is a small exhibition on the work's conceptualisation, fabrication and installation, including a scale model.

Lightning with Stag in its Glare

Created by German artist Joseph Beuys, this installation's suspended bronze triangle represents a bolt of lightning illuminating various startled animals. The three-wheeled cart represents a goat and the upended ironing board a stag. It's Beuys' only metallic work.

How Profound Is The Air

This permanent exhibit is the work of San Sebastián native Eduardo Chillida, who studied architecture in Madrid before taking up art. It is sculpted from alabaster, juxtaposing a rough natural-stone exterior and highly polished interior.

Temporary Exhibitions

The museum's exceptional temporary shows – from retrospectives of the groundbreaking contemporary video artist Bill Viola to wide-ranging exhibitions that explore *fin de siècle* Paris – are the main attraction for many visitors.

Top Experience 📷
Watch Athletic Bilbao on their Home Ground

◎ MAP P62, A3

www.athletic-club.eus

Catching a game at the Estadio San Mamés with thousands of avid fans is quite the Bilbao cultural experience. The home side, Athletic Bilbao, is one of Spain's most successful clubs, and one of only three to have never been relegated from La Liga, along with Real Madrid and Barcelona.

Athletic Bilbao

The club, founded in 1898 after British sailors introduced football to the city, inspires passionate local support, and its traditional red and white colours are displayed in cafes and bars across town. But what sets it apart – and makes its achievements even more impressive – is its unique policy of only signing Basque players. Tickets for games are available through the team's website, directly at the stadium or, on match days, from BKK cashpoint machines.

Museum

A must for all AC Bilbao fans, high-tech museum **Museo Athletic Club** (www.athletic-club.eus) delves into the club's legendary past, with gear and trophies dating back to 1905. Interactive touchscreens allow you to see game highlights over the last half century. For the full experience, tack on a 45-minute stadium tour (English available) that takes you to the press room, the changing rooms and out onto the pitch.

Pre or Post-Match Drink

Get into the Athletic Bilbao spirit with a pre- or post-match celebratory drink at La Peña Athletic (p47). This old town bar, filled with red and white vintage tops, trophies and team photos, is the place to go to hang out with enthusiastic local fans.

★ Top Tips

o Tickets are best bought online from the official site athletic-club.eus

o You can also buy tickets at San Mamés Stadium ticket offices, open from the day before the match up until kick-off.

o Tickets for the museum and stadium tours can also be bought online in advance.

o Learn more by picking up an audio guide (included in adult admission) at the museum entrance.

✕ Take a Break

Enjoy *pintxos*, menus of the day and drinks at the stadium's on-site tavern, **La Campa de los Ingleses** (www.es.lacampadelosingleses.com; 📶).

There's also the more formal **San Mamés Jatetxea** (www.sanmamesjatetxea.com), where chef Fernando Canales serves up Basque classics.

Walking Tour

Go on an Architecture Tour of the New Town

Bilbao rewards those who take the time to walk its streets admiring the contrasting collections of architectural styles, enjoying the riverside walkways and passing plenty of places where you can sample a drink and pintxo or two. This walk takes you past the most memorable historic and contemporary buildings in the city.

Walk Facts

Start Concordia train station; M Abando

Finish Abando train station; M Abando

Length 7km; three hours

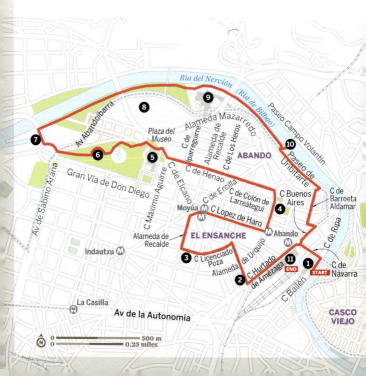

❶ Concordia Train Station

Start at one of the city's architectural treasures, the 1902-built **Concordia train station**, with its beautifully tiled art-nouveau facade.

❷ Teatro Campos Elíseos

Another art-nouveau beauty, the **Teatro Campos Elíseos** (p70), also dates from 1902. Since its restoration in 2010, it stages theatre and musical performances.

❸ Sede de Sanidad del Gobierno Vasco

The headquarters of the Basque Health Department was only completed in 2008, but has since become a striking city landmark. Created from sheets of glass and steel, this multifaceted building was designed by Juan Coll-Barreu.

❹ Jardines Albia

The leafy Jardines Albia, overlooked by the 16th-century Iglesia San Vicente Mártir, are a peaceful spot to rest up, with a fountain at the gardens' centre.

❺ Museo de Bellas Artes

A 1945-built neoclassical building, added to in 1970 and in 1996, it houses the fine arts museum, the **Museo de Bellas Artes** (p70).

❻ Parque de Doña Casilda de Iturrizar

Stroll through the **Parque de Doña Casilda de Iturrizar** (p65) with its bandstands and duck ponds.

❼ Itsasmuseum

To get a sense of Bilbao's industrial past, stop outside the city's maritime museum, the **Itsasmuseum** (p64). On the western side, opposite the dry docks, you'll see the bright-red 'Carola' crane (1957) formerly used for shipbuilding.

❽ Torre Iberdrola

Rising from the southern bank, the obelisk-like Torre Iberdrola is a 165m-high, 41-storey glinting glass office block. Inaugurated in 2012, it's the tallest building in the region.

❾ Museo Guggenheim Bilbao

Head to the city's most famous building, the **Museo Guggenheim Bilbao** (p54) – a titanium masterpiece that changed perceptions of modern architecture when it opened in 1997. Outside, check out iconic sculptures including Louise Bourgeois' spider-like *Maman* and Jeff Koons' flower-adorned *Puppy*.

❿ Puente Zubizuri

Continue upriver to the Puente Zubizuri, the striking wave-like bridge designed by Santiago Calatrava.

⓫ Estación de Abando

Finish up your tour by heading inside **Abando train station** where you'll see a huge stained glass window depicting typical Basque scenes of farmers, fishermen and industrial workers.

Bilbao New Town

For reviews see

- ⦿ Top Experiences — p54
- ⦾ Sights — p64
- ⊗ Eating — p65
- 🅟 Drinking — p68
- ⭑ Entertainment — p70
- 🅐 Shopping — p71

Map locations:
- 4 Bilbobentura
- 1 Itsasmuseum
- 28 Euskalduna
- 38 Abandoibarra
- 6 Parque de Doña Casilda de Iturrizar
- Museo de Bellas Artes
- Estadio San Mamés
- 34
- 15, 13
- 18
- 32
- 35 Plaza Arriquibar
- 23
- 31, 2 Azkuna Zentroa

Streets and landmarks: Av Madariaga, Deustoarrak, Ría del Nervión (Ría de Bilbao), Pedro Arrupe Footbridge, Universidad de Deusto, C Evaristo Churrca, Av Abandoibarra, Guggenheim, C Lehendakari Leizaola, Alameda Mazarredo, Plaza del Museo, C de Elcano, Parque de la Misericordia, Gran Vía de Don Diego, C Máximo Aguirre, C de Iparraguirre, Sabino Arana, C de Rodríguez Arias, Plaza de Campuzano, C de Licenciado Poza, C de Ercilla, San Mamés, Alameda de Urquijo, Indautxu, Plaza de Indautxu, Alameda de Recalde, Alameda de San Mamés, C de Luis Briñas, Av de Sabino Arana, C de María Díaz de Haro, Alameda Doctor Areilza, C Manuel Allende, C de Gregorio de la Revilla, Plaza de Echnaniz, Basurto, La Casilla, Plaza de la Casilla, Av de la Autonomía, C General Salazar

Bilbao New Town

63

- Bilbao ✈ (11km)
- C de las Universidades
- 🔴 Museo Guggenheim Bilbao
- 12 ✕
- Av Maurice Ravel
- C Castaños
- C Huertas de la Villa
- 7 ⦿ Funicular de Artxanda
- Paseo Campo Volantin
- C Lersundi
- 17
- Alameda Mazarredo
- 19
- C Barrainqua
- C de Cosme Echevarrieta
- 22 ✕
- C de Los Heros
- C de Uribitarte
- Uribitarte 🚇
- Paseo de Uribitarte
- 5 ⦿ Zubizuri
- Alameda de Recalde
- C de Ercilla
- 37 🛏
- 10 ✕
- Plaza de Jado
- Plaza del Ensanche
- **ABANDO**
- C Ibañez de Bilbao
- 25 ✕
- C San Vicente
- 30
- 3 ⦿ Bilboats
- Pio Baroja
- Av Zumalacárregui
- Plaza de Colón de Larreátegui
- C de Barroeta Aldamar
- 14 ✕
- Puente del Ayuntamiento
- 🚇 Moyúa
- C de Ledesma
- 20 ✕
- Plaza Venezuela
- Parque de Etxebarria
- Buses to Bilbao airport
- 9 ✕
- Gran Vía López de Haro
- C de la Diputación
- C Berástegui
- C Buenos Aires
- 21
- C Príncipe
- 8 ✕
- **EL ENSANCHE**
- Abando 🚇
- 36 🛏
- 33
- 16
- Plaza del Arenal
- C Esperanza
- C de General Concha
- Alameda de Urquijo
- Abando 🚇
- C de Navarra
- Puente del Arenal
- C de Arenal
- 🚇 Casco Viejo
- C de Elcano
- Alameda de Amézaga
- Abando Train Station (Renfe)
- Plaza Circular (Plaza de España)
- Concordia Train Station
- Plaza Arriaga
- Plaza Nueva
- Euskalduna
- 27 ⦿
- C Hurtado de Amézaga
- Arriaga
- C Jardines
- **CASCO VIEJO**
- 11
- 24
- C Bailén
- Ría del Nervión (Ría de Bilbao)
- C de la Cruz
- Plaza de Zabalburu
- C de García Salazar
- C Lamana
- Puente de la Merced
- 29
- Las Siete Calles
- Juan de Garay Kalea
- C C Hernani
- M de la Merced
- Ribera 🚇
- C de Somera
- C de San Francisco

Sights

Itsasmuseum MUSEUM
1 MAP P62, A2

On the waterfront, this interactive maritime museum brings the watery depths of Bilbao and Basque maritime history to life. Start with a 10-minute video for an overview of Bilbao history, from the 1300s to the present before wandering through the two floors of displays, which show old shipbuilding techniques, harrowing shipwrecks (and innovative coastal rescue strategies), pirate threats and intricate models – including a full-scale recreation of the 1511 Consulate Barge. Outdoors, you can clamber about a range of boats. (www.itsasmuseum.eus; 👬)

Azkuna Zentroa ARCHITECTURE
2 MAP P62, D5

Take a neglected wine storage warehouse, convert it into a leisure and cultural centre, add a shot of Bilbao style and the result is the Azkuna Zentroa (also known as Alhóndiga). Repurposed by renowned architect Philippe Starck, it now houses a cinema, art gallery, rooftop swimming pool with a glass bottom, a public media centre, cafes and restaurants.

The ground floor is notable for its 43 tubby columns, each constructed with a unique design symbolising infinite cultures, architecture, wars and religion. (www.azkunazentroa.eus)

Bilboats BOATING
3 MAP P62, G3

See the city from a different perspective by taking a boat tour along the Ría del Nervión and getting a unique view of its architectural splendours.

Bilboats offers two routes – either one-hour or two-hour.

The one-hour tour (adults €14, children five–10 €10, kids under five €1) around the New Town takes in sights such as the Zubizuri Bridge and the Guggenheim.

The second option follows the same route over two hours (adults €19, children five–10 €14, kids under five €1), taking you all the way up to the famous Puente Colcada (Hanging Bridge) in Portugalete. (www.bilboats.com)

Bilbobentura WATER SPORTS
4 MAP P62, A2

This dockside outfit hires out single and double kayaks and SUP boards.

It also offers various group outings, including evening paddles and daytime tours.

Life jackets and waterproof bags are included; lockers and changing rooms are available at the premises. (www.bilbobentura.com)

Zubizuri BRIDGE
5 MAP P62, G2

The most striking of the modern bridges that span the Ría del Nervión, the Zubizuri (Basque for 'White Bridge') has become an iconic feature of Bilbao's cityscape since its completion in 1997.

The work of Spanish architect Santiago Calatrava, it has a curved glass-brick walkway (slippery when wet) suspended under a flowing white arch to which it's attached by a series of steel spokes.

Parque de Doña Casilda de Iturrizar   PARK

6 ◉ MAP P62, C3

Planted with maples, lindens, cedars, palms and 70 other species of trees, the Parque de Doña Casilda de Iturrizar was completed in 1920.

The centrepiece of this elegant, English-style park is the small pond filled with ducks and swans.

Funicular de Artxanda   FUNICULAR

7 ◉ MAP P62, G1

Bilbao is a city hemmed in by hills and mountains, resting in a tight valley. For a breathtaking view over the city and the wild Basque mountains beyond, take a trip on the funicular railway that has creaked its way up the steep slope to the summit of Artxanda since 1915. (www.funicularartxanda.bilbao.eus)

Eating

La Viña del Ensanche   PINTXOS €€

8 ◉ MAP P62, E4

With old-fashioned, wood-panelled walls and framed postcards written by adoring fans over the years,

Funicular de Artxanda

Bilbao's Background

Bilbao was granted the title of *villa* (city-state) in 1300 and medieval *bilbaínos* went about their business in the bustle of **Las Siete Calles** (p41), the original seven streets of the old town, and down on the wharves. The conquest of the Americas stimulated trade and Basque fishers, merchants and settlers soon built strong links to cities such as Boston. By the late 19th century, the smokestacks of steelworks, shipbuilding yards and chemical plants dominated the area's skyline.

From the Carlist Wars through to the Spanish Civil War, Bilbao was always considered the greatest prize in the north, largely for its industrial value. Franco took the city in the spring of 1937 and reprisals against Basque nationalists were massive and long lasting. Yet during the Franco era, the city prospered as it fed Spanish industrial needs. This was followed by the seemingly terminal economic decline that has been so dynamically reversed since the mid 1990s, as Bilbao has transitioned to a service-based economy and a tourist and cultural hotspot.

La Viña del Ensanche maintains a reputation as one of Bilbao's best eating spots – no small achievement for a place that has been in business since 1927. Mouthwatering morsels of ham, seared mackerel and crispy asparagus tempura are just a few of the many temptations. (www.lavinadelensanche.com)

El Globo PINTXOS €

9 MAP P62, E4

One of Bilbao's best *pintxos* bars, El Globo packs a fabulous range of creative small bites, including favourites such as *txangurro gratinado* (spider crab) and *hongos con su crema y crujiente de jamón* (mushrooms with crispy ham). Its congenial atmosphere and central location draw a wide cross-section of locals and visitors. Go early to beat the crowds. (www.barelglobo.es)

Zortziko GASTRONOMY €€€

10 MAP P62, F3

Smoked cauliflower with caviar; plankton ravioli with apple-pepper gel; grilled scallops with citrus foam and yucca; Iberian pork cheeks stewed in Pedro Ximenez wine; and white chocolate, vanilla and peach semifreddo are just a few of the highly technical creations on this elegant Michelin-starred restaurant's tasting menus. There's also a special barbecue/grill menu (€240 for two). Book well ahead. (www.zortziko.es)

Casa Rufo
BASQUE €€

11 MAP P62, F5

Tucked in the back of a small deli and wine shop, Casa Rufo feels like a hidden dining spot – albeit one that's terrible at keeping secrets (reserve ahead). Amid shelves packed with top-quality wines, diners tuck into delectable Navarran asparagus, house-smoked duck, baked cod with tomatoes and red peppers, and chargrilled steaks. (www.casarufo.com)

Nerua Guggenheim Bilbao
BASQUE €€€

12 MAP P62, E1

The Museo Guggenheim Bilbao's Michelin-starred, modernist, white and ultraminimalist restaurant is under the direction of chef Josean Alija (a disciple of Ferran Adrià). Needless to say, the *nueva cocina vasca* (Basque nouvelle cuisine) is breathtaking, with multicourse extravaganzas that you'll be remembering (and perhaps paying for) long after you return home. There are also à la carte options, besides the tasting menu. (www.neruaguggenheimbilbao.com)

El Puertito
SEAFOOD €

13 MAP P62, D4

On warm summer evenings, wine-sipping crowds congregate at this small bar to enjoy an oyster or six, accompanied by a glass of crisp local white wine. Choose from a chalked-up menu of Galician, French and Portuguese oysters, served simply with a squeeze of lemon (or Tabasco sauce on request). (www.elpuertito.es)

Bascook
BASQUE €€

14 MAP P62, G3

Occupying a former salt warehouse, this low-lit space with exposed stone walls and elegantly set tables makes an atmospheric backdrop for high-end cooking. Chef Aitor Elizegi earns rave reviews for creative dishes such as cod *pil pil* with kimchi, baked egg with truffle Parmentier, mushrooms and asparagus, and roast duck with orange peel and fig chutney. (www.bascook.com;)

Yandiola
BASQUE €€€

Inside Bilbao's Azkuna Zentroa (Alhóndiga) cultural centre, Yandiola (see 2 Map p62, D5) features modern Basque and Spanish fare that is as highly touted as the strikingly redeveloped building itself.

Among the many hits are grilled mushrooms with egg yolk and a black garlic emulsion, pigeon risotto, and grilled cod cheeks.

Arrive early – or stick around afterwards – for a drink on the roof terrace. (www.yandiola.com)

El Huevo Frito
PINTXOS €

15 MAP P62, D4

The bar at this relaxed, casual spot is laden with bright red-and-yellow Ortiz seafood tins beneath slate tiles that display its tempting array of *pintxos*.

> ### Dine at Basquery
>
>
> Equal parts cafe, bakery, microbrewery and dining destination, the postindustrial, multiroom **Basquery** (Map p62, G4; www.basquery.com) has a stunning line-up of daily dishes, from traditional and vegan burgers to pizzas, plus appetisers such as fried artichokes with parmesan, and nachos that pair perfectly with the in-house IPA, golden ale and session stout. They also serve delectable homemade buttery pastries and topped toasts for breakfast. Its deli, stocking tinned fish, preserved veggies and more, is next door.

Most feature the bar's eponymous 'fried egg', such as *morcilla* (blood sausage), tempura cod with chorizo, and *jamón ibérico* (Iberian ham), each topped with a quail's egg.

La Camelia VEGAN €€

18 MAP P62, G4

On a mostly pedestrian lane near the bridge to the old town, La Camelia serves up excellent vegan fare, including quinoa tabbouleh, tofu or seitan wraps, a range of delicious burgers and *maki sushi* (rice and vegetables rolled in seaweed).

Service can be slow, so plan on lingering over a few drinks at the outdoor tables before your meal arrives. (www.lacameliaveganbar.com;)

Singular PINTXOS €€

17 MAP P62, F2

Amid rough-hewn stone walls, vintage iron columns, sleek industrial pipes and venting, and bare-bulbed lights, Singular lays out bite-size morsels of pure perfection on its marble-topped bar.

Enjoy high-quality *raciones* such as tuna belly in olive oil, leeks in vinegarette and cheese platters, which you can complement with a craft brew (eight on tap and another 50 by the bottle). (www.singularbar.com)

Drinking

Cork WINE BAR

18 MAP P62, C4

Taste your way around some of Spain's finest small artisan vineyards at this cosy wine bar owned and run by Jonathan García, a former Basque sommelier champion. Its blackboard chalks up 25 whites and 40 reds available by the glass. Selections change every two months but always include lightly sparkling *txakoli* and rich reds from La Rioja. (www.corkbilbao.com)

Gin Fizz COCKTAIL BAR

19 MAP P62, F2

Back-lit cabinets and contemporary furnishings make this a stylish place for sipping cocktails such as its namesake, Gin Fizz (gin, sugar syrup and soda), or Pearls & Roses (jasmine and rose petal–infused gin with orange blossom water and Agua del Carmen tonic, topped with cream). Other gin infusions include green tea and liquorice, and dehydrated strawberries and chocolate. (www.ginfizzbilbaococktail.com)

Café Iruña   CAFE

20 MAP P62, F4

Moorish-style arches, exquisite tiling, polychrome wooden ceilings, frescoes and a marble bar are the defining characteristics of this grande dame dating from 1903. Still a wonderful place for people-watching, it works as well for afternoon coffee or an evening drink as it does for breakfast, lunch (don't miss the delicious *pinchos morunos*; spicy lamb kebabs) or dinner. (www.cafeirunabilbao.net)

Baobab   CAFE

21 MAP P62, G4

When the rains arrive, cosy Baobab is a fine place to retreat. This riverside cafe has an excellent array of teas, infusions, beer, wine, vermouth and snacks; everything is organic and fair trade. Works by local artists regularly cover the walls, and there's a regular line-up of acoustic jam sessions, poetry readings and more. (www.baobabteteria.com)

Residence   BAR

22 MAP P62, E2

Residence hosts acoustic jam sessions throughout the month, including Irish folk, blues and roots. Even when there's nothing on, it's a great little spot for a whisky, with more than 200 varieties to choose from, or a Manhattan cocktail (rye whisky, vermouth and bitters) and a chat with the friendly bar staff. (www.residencecafe.com)

Cotton Club   CLUB

23 MAP P62, C5

A Bilbao institution since 1994, with a saxophone beer tap and bottle cap–studded walls, the Cotton Club draws a diverse crowd to its DJ-stoked nights and regular gigs – mainly jazz, blues and rock. It's a tiny place so prepare to get up close with your fellow revellers. (www.cottonclubbilbao.es)

El Balcón de la Lola   CLUB

24 MAP P62, F5

Located under the railway lines, El Balcón de la Lola doesn't get going until late. One of Bilbao's most popular mixed gay/straight clubs, this is the place to end the night if you want to keep the weekend party rolling till daybreak. It has industrial decor and packs in dance lovers – the music is mostly house.

See the Masterpieces at the Museo de Bellas Artes

The **Museo de Bellas Artes** (Map p62, D3; www.museobilbao.com) houses a compelling collection that includes everything from Gothic sculptures to 20th-century pop art. There are three main subcollections: classical art, with works by Murillo, Zurbarán, El Greco, Goya and Van Dyck; contemporary art, featuring works by Gauguin, Francis Bacon and Anthony Caro; and Basque art, with works of the great sculptors Jorge Oteiza and Eduardo Chillida, and strong paintings by the likes of Ignacio Zuloaga and Juan de Echevarría.

It's currently undergoing a massive renovation that will take a couple of years, so some rooms will be closed, but while that's going on entrance is free.

Cinnamon CAFE
25 MAP P62, G3

Billing itself as a 'coffee lab', Cinnamon brews organic, Basque-roasted beans in a spectrum of styles, and also serves fresh juices, smoothies, herbal and loose-leaf teas, and craft beers. Alongside its drinks list, its 'urban food' spans brunch dishes and pastries to salads and open-faced sandwiches. Vintage mismatched furniture and fittings fill the postindustrial space. (www.facebook.com/cinnamonbilbao; 🛜)

Entertainment

Kafe Antzokia LIVE MUSIC
26 MAP P62, G3

Within a former cinema, this is the vibrant heart of contemporary Basque Bilbao, featuring international rock, blues and reggae, as well as the cream of Basque rock-pop. There are weekend concerts, followed by DJs until the early hours. During the day, it's a cafe, restaurant and cultural centre with Basque dancing classes (sign up online) all rolled into one. (www.kafeantzokia.eus)

Teatro Campos Elíseos THEATRE
27 MAP P62, F5

Restored to its art-nouveau glory and modernised for contemporary productions in 2010, this showpiece was built in 1902. Today, the magnificent venue hosts plays, musicals, dance, concerts, comedy, puppet and magic shows, and occasional cinema screenings. Its multitiered main hall has a capacity of 805, while the more intimate, top-floor dome room accommodates 250 people. (www.teatrocampos.com)

Euskalduna Palace LIVE MUSIC
28 MAP P62, B2

Built on the riverside former shipyards in 1999, in a style that echoes the great shipbuilding works of the 19th century, this vast venue is home to the Bilbao Symphony Orchestra and the Basque Symphony Orchestra. With a 2164-capacity main hall and 18 smaller halls, it hosts a wide array of operas, concerts, musicals and films. (www.euskalduna.eus)

Bilborock   LIVE MUSIC

29 MAP P62, G6

Spectacularly set in a 17th-century former church, La Merced, with soaring tiered seating and a ceiling dome, this multipurpose venue is best known for its rock, metal and pop-rock concerts. Bilborock also has film screenings, plays, poetry readings and workshops. (www.facebook.com/bilborockaretoa)

Back & Stage   LIVE MUSIC

30 MAP P62, G3

This popular venue incorporates two separate spaces, Stage Live and the Back Room. Along with local and international bands, it hosts DJs and various parties; check the website to see what's on while you're here. (www.backandstage.com)

Shopping

DendAZ   DESIGN

31 MAP P62, D5

Emerging and established Basque artists and designers showcase their works at this retail space within the Azkuna Zentroa (p64) cultural centre. Browse for contemporary clothing,

Euskalduna Palace

including arty T-shirts, shoes and hats, as well as bags, jewellery, artworks, lamps, cabinets, ceramics and stationery. The space is regularly reconfigured to display the rotating stock, so it's worth popping in to see the latest directions in Basque design. (http://dendaz.azkunazentroa.eus)

Chocolates de Mendaro   CHOCOLATE

32 MAP P62, D4

This old-time chocolate shop spills over with pralines, truffles and nougats in shapes including anchovies and oysters, and stocks its own hot chocolate mixes.

It was founded in 1850 by the Saint-Gerons family, who installed a cocoa mill at their rural property, where chocolates are still made by hand today. Visits to the mill are possible by appointment. (www.chocolatesdemendaro.com)

Power Records   MUSIC

33 MAP P62, G4

This record shop has been a point of reference for Bilbao's vinyl lovers since the mid-1990s.

Its encyclopaedic collection runs the gamut from death metal to Shirley Bassey by way of salsa, jazz, rock, pop and blues. There are LPs, posters, CDs and collectors' box sets. (www.powerrecords-bilbao.com)

La Oka   FOOD & DRINKS

34 MAP P62, C4

This swish deli and boutique food shop sells a range of traditional northern Spanish and Basque products from cheeses and wines to jars of *guindilla* peppers and tinned seafood.

There's also a counter for fresh produce as well as homemade dishes to take away. (www.laoka.es)

Crosta Ogitegia-Enkarterri Concept Store   FOOD & DRINKS

35 MAP P62, D4

Products at this little bakery are all sourced from the mountain-

---

Universidad de Deusto

Over the river from the Museo Guggenheim Bilbao, and accessible via the Pedro Arrupe footbridge, the **Universidad de Deusto** (Map p62, D1; www.deusto.es) dominates the northern riverfront. This landmark building, initially one of Bilbao's largest, was designed by architect Francisco de Cubas in 1886 to house the Jesuit Deusto university. To the southwest of the university, Deusto is a largely residential district. But if you're in the area and fancy a bite, **Deustoarrak** (Map p62, B1; www.deustoarrak.com) is one of a number of restaurants on the neighbourhood's central strip, Avenida Madariaga.

ous rural municipality of Enkarterri to Bilbao's west. Along with sourdough loaves baked daily in a wood-fired oven, it stocks cheeses, cured meats, pastries, vinegar, oils, jams, honey, wine, craft beers and chocolate.

Persuade — FASHION & ACCESSORIES
36 MAP P62, G4

A former warehouse with timber beams, exposed brick walls and cast-iron columns makes an inspiring backdrop for browsing cutting-edge fashion by top international designers, such as Yohji Yamamoto, Daniela Gregis and Bernhard Willhelm.

You'll find one-off creations, as well as vintage clothing, hats and bags. (www.persuade.es)

Market — HOMEWARES
37 MAP P62, E3

The miscellany of wares at this imaginative homewares shop includes plant-filled terrariums, geometric ceramic pots, antique furniture, and artisan soaps and skincare products from Bilbao-based Xaboi Punpuila. (www.facebook.com/marketbilbao)

Bilbao's Modern Metro

Bilbao's architectural riches run deep. Walk across town and you'll come across a number of futuristic glass-and-steel constructions emerging from the ground. Nicknamed *fosteritos* after Sir Norman Foster, the British architect who designed them between 1988 and 1995, these are the entrances to the clean, cavernous stations of Bilbao's three-line metro system – a masterpiece of modern functional design.

Zubiarte — SHOPPING CENTRE
38 MAP P62, C2

Overlooking the river by the Deusto bridge, this impressive brick, stone and glass shopping centre was designed by US architect Robert Stern in 2004.

Inside, some 50 shops include Zara, H&M and other well-known stores.

Also here are a supermarket, food court and an eight-screen cinema. (www.zubiarte.com)

Explore
Getxo & Portugalete

Consisting of five separate districts, the municipality of Getxo has sandy beaches, waterfront promenades and seafood restaurants. Across the river is Portugalete's compact medieval centre.

The Short List

○ **Puente Colgante (p80)** *Gliding across the Unesco-listed transporter bridge linking Gexto and Portugalete.*

○ **Basílica de Santa María (p80)** *Stepping inside Portugalete's 16th-century Gothic basilica to admire its carved altarpiece.*

○ **Rialia Museo de la Industria (p80)** *Delving into Portugalete's industrial past at this intriguing museum.*

○ **Playa de Ereaga (p82)** *Soaking up the sun on this sheltered Gexto beach.*

○ **Bar Arrantzale (p85)** *Sipping wine on the cobbled terrace of this bar in Puerto Viejo's atmospheric old fishing village.*

Getting There & Around

[M] To reach Getxo, take Metro Bilbao's Línea 1, with key stops at Areeta, Neguri and Algorta.

[M] Portugalete is served by Línea 2 (Portugalete stop).

Getxo & Portugalete Map on p78

Gexto Port MIMADEO/SHUTTERSTOCK ©

Walking Tour

Go on a Seaside Ramble in Getxo

An easy metro ride from Bilbao, the seaside district of Getxo offers a serene escape from the city. Clifftop views, a pretty beach and the charming, narrow lanes of an old fishing village make for an enchanting afternoon wander. There are also plenty of opportunities for snacking along the way, so come with an appetite.

Walk Facts

Start Aixerrota Windmill; M Bidezabal

Finish San Nicolás de Bari; M Algorta

Length 2km; two hours

❶ Aixerrota Windmill

Begin your walk along this beautiful stretch of coast by admiring the windmill here, which was built to counter drought-affected watermills and was in operation from 1726 until 1787. It's not currently open to visitors, but is still interesting to admire from the outside.

❷ Playa de Arrigunaga

Near the mouth of the Nervión estuary, the **Playa de Arrigunaga** is a lovely stretch of beachfront, backed by steep hillside. This is a great spot to slow down and take in the scene, with skaters zipping around on a skate park near the centre of the beach, and surfers out on the waves.

❸ Parque Usategi

High up on the cliffs above the sea, the small Parque Usategi is frequented by joggers, dog-walkers, families (there's a kids' playground) and strollers, who enjoy a quiet pocket of Getxo graced with sea breezes. It overlooks **Jeffrey's Surf Spot**, a favourite with local surfers thanks to waves of up to 3m (conditions permitting).

❹ Puerto Viejo

Puerto Viejo (p87) feels like a vestige of another era. Steep, narrow lanes skirt past stone cottages decorated with brightly painted green shutters and balconies draped with hanging plants. Once the domain of sailors and fisherfolk, the small seaside community remains tightly knit, with children playing in the streets and old friends gathering over drinks at sundown.

❺ Txomin Taberna

Wander through the atmospheric lanes of Puerto Viejo to find neighbourhood charmer **Txomin Taberna**. Try a Sarracena wheat beer, made by local microbrewer Tito Blas, along with tasty *pintxos* (croquettes, anchovies, mussels in tomato salsa).

❻ Plaza de San Nicolás

Away from the seafront, the Plaza de San Nicolás is one of the prettiest squares in Getxo. It's also a completely local scene, with a handful of outdoor cafes. It's liveliest in the afternoons, when adults gather for an aperitif, while young ones chase one another about the square.

❼ San Nicolás de Bari

Built between 1854 and 1863 by Lorenzo Fancisco de Móñiz and refurbished in 1925 in neoclassical style, **San Nicolás de Bari**, on the square's northwestern side, has a stepped belfry. It's dedicated to the patron saint of sailors; an exquisite model ship hangs above the altar.

Sights

Puente Colgante BRIDGE

1 ⊙ MAP P78, E6

Designed by Alberto Palacio, a disciple of Gustave Eiffel, the Unesco World Heritage–listed Puente Colgante (also known as the Vizcaya or Bizkaia Bridge) was the world's first transporter bridge, opened in 1883. The bridge, which links Getxo and Portugalete, consists of a suspended platform that sends cars and passengers gliding silently over the Ría del Nervión. You can take a lift up to the superstructure walkway at 46m and walk across for some great, though decidedly breezy, views. (www.puente-colgante.com)

Basílica de Santa María BASILICA

2 ⊙ MAP P78, F8

Portugalete's impressive basilica (1580) stands atop an earlier 14th-century church that originally marked the town's highest point. A striking structure, it's largely Gothic with flying buttresses, gargoyles and austere sandstone walls; the bell tower was a later 18th-century addition. Inside, the carved wood Renaissance-era altarpiece is a highlight.

Plaza del Solar SQUARE

3 ⊙ MAP P78, F7

At the foot of Portugalete's medieval centre, this cobbled square makes for a fine photo with its handsome 19th-century buildings and august monument to Víctor Chávarri (1854–1900), a local industrialist, business person and politician. At the plaza's heart, an ornate bandstand provides the outdoor stage for regular Sunday performances by the local brass band.

Rialia Museo de la Industría MUSEUM

4 ⊙ MAP P78, C8

Learn about Portugalete's industrial history at this small waterfront museum. Displays, which include paintings, models and machinery parts, chart the town's development and the effect early industrialisation had on the area's landscape and social make-

Plaza del Solar

Puente Colgante (p80)

up. Best of all are the short films showing fiery industrial action – smelting, welding, molten flows – backed by dramatic musical arrangements.

Paseo de las Grandes Villas   AREA

5 ◎ MAP P78, D5

The Paseo is the unofficial name given to Getxo's seafront – made up of Muelle de Las Arenas Areeta and Calle Marques de Arriluce e Ibarra.

The 'Villas' part of the name is a reference to the extravagant mansions that pepper the route, many of which date to the town's heyday in the early 20th century.

Two to look out for are the 1911-built **Casa Cisco** and turreted, early-20th-century **Lezama-Legizamón**.

Galerías de Punta Begoña   LANDMARK

6 ◎ MAP P78, D3

This massive stone structure was built in 1919 as a continuation of Getxo's defensive wall. It's an impressive sight, complete with columns and a balustraded terrace, though it's in a bad state of decay. Long-term restoration, however, is underway. And while it's not all open to the public, free one-hour guided visits in Basque and Spanish are offered throughout the year, with some English-language tours in August. (www.puntabegonagetxo.eus)

Playa de Ereaga　　　　　　BEACH

7 🎯 MAP P78, D2

Ideal for families, this long, sheltered sandy beach runs between the Galerías de Punta Begoña and Puerto Viejo. You can hire sunbeds and parasols. Beach football (soccer) tournaments take place here in summer.

El Bote　　　　　　　　　　CRUISE

8 🎯 MAP P78, F8

El Bote runs a circular hop-on, hop-off route from Portugalete, passing under the Puente Colgante (p80), up to Santurtzi (on the Nervión's west bank), across to Getxo's El Abra Marina and back (there are also trips back to Bilbao). Multilingual audio guides are included. The boat sails three times per day (four in August), with the first departure at 11.15am. There are also *pintxo* cruises. (www.elbotebilbao.com)

Eating

Jai Alai　　　　　　　　　　BASQUE €

9 ❌ MAP P78, D6

Chic, modern *pintxo* bar with creative bites such as *morcilla* (black pudding) with quail egg, grilled octopus with aioli and squid-ink *croqueta*. It also has classic sharing rations such as scallops, cheese boards and *txistorra* sausage, as well as some international ones like nachos and barbecue chicken wings.

Karola Etxea　　　　　SEAFOOD €€€

10 ❌ MAP P78, A1

The blue-trimmed, wood-beamed dining room of this Puerto Viejo restaurant, atmospherically housed in a picture-perfect, white fisher's cottage, sets the stage for delicacies such as fresh prawns, scallops, hake and clams in green sauce, and *txangurro* (baked spider crab). While seafood is the speciality, there are also a couple of daily meat dishes. (www.karolaetxea.net)

Tamarises Izarra　　　　BASQUE €€€

11 ❌ MAP P78, D2

Basque chef Javier Izarra's creative contemporary cuisine earns him rave reviews. At his smart beachside premises' formal upstairs

Puerto Viejo, Gexto (p87)

A Basque History Lesson

No one quite knows where the Basque people came from (they have no migration myth in their oral history), but their presence here is believed to predate even the earliest known migrations.

The Romans left the hilly Basque Country more or less to itself, but the expansionist Castilian crown gained sovereignty over Basque territories during the Middle Ages (1000–1450), although with considerable difficulty; Navarra constituted a separate kingdom until 1512.

Even when they came within the Castilian orbit, Navarra and the three other Basque provinces (Guipúzcoa, Vizcaya and Álava) extracted broad autonomy arrangements, known as the *fueros* (the ancient laws of the Basques).

After the Second Carlist War in 1876, all provinces except Navarra were stripped of their coveted *fueros*, thereby fuelling nascent Basque nationalism.

Yet, although the Partido Nacionalista Vasco (PNV; Basque Nationalist Party) was established in 1894, support was never uniform as all Basque provinces included a considerable Castilian contingent.

When the Republican government in Madrid proposed the possibility of home rule (self-government) to the Basques in 1936, both Guipúzcoa and Vizcaya took up the offer.

When the Spanish Civil War erupted, conservative rural Navarra and Álava supported Franco, while Vizcaya and Guipúzcoa sided with the Republicans, a decision they paid a high price for in the four decades that followed.

It was during the Franco days that Euskadi Ta Askatasuna (ETA; Basque Homeland and Freedom) was first born. It was originally set up to fight against the Franco regime, which suppressed the Basques through banning the language and almost all forms of Basque culture.

After Franco's death, ETA called for nothing less than total independence and continued its bloody fight against the Spanish government until, in October 2011, the group announced a 'definitive cessation of its armed activity'.

Today, while ETA is no longer active, there is still a peaceful but strong sense of nationalism, and you'll often see banners, posters and signs emblazoned with the words *Euskal Herriak Independentzia* (Basque Country Independence) throughout the region.

Punta Galea

Walking path **Paseo de Punta Galea** runs for 6km around the Punta Galea, the cliff-bound promontory that juts into the sea north of Getxo, characterised by its exposed rock strata and white cliffs similar to those of Normandy, France, and Dover, England.

At the path's southern end is the 18th-century **Aixerrota Windmill** and 1km north are the remains of **Fuerte de La Galea**, a defensive fort dating from 1742.

The path's northernmost point is **Playa Salvaje**, where you'll often see airborne paragliders. If you're keen to take to the skies yourself, book a tandem paragliding flight with **Parapente** (www.parapentesopelana.com) for spectacular aerial views of the coast's geological formations and beaches.

For a quick return to Getxo (and Bilbao), hop on Metro Bilbao's Línea 1 at Larrabasterra, 1.2km southeast of Playa Salvaje.

---

restaurant and sunny sea-facing terrace, you can dine on innovative creations such as red shrimp tartare with a prawn smoothie, followed by *marmitako* (Basque seafood stew) with lobster, finishing off with pear puff pastry with creamy noisette butter ice cream. (www.tamarisesizarra.com)

Punta Malabata INTERNATIONAL €€

13 MAP P78, E6

Set on the riverfront near the Puente Colgante, this chic contemporary restaurant serves up a range of international bites from Vietnamese-style chicken salad and Nordic-style open sandwiches with salmon, avocado, boiled egg and crab, to vegan burgers, noodles and bao buns.

Vegetarian and gluten-free options available. They also have a good selection of beers. (www.puntamalabata.es)

La Kazuela BASQUE €€

13 MAP P78, C6

A few streets from the historic Puente Colgante transporter bridge, this lively bar-restaurant is popular for *pintxos* – the salmon and Cantabrian anchovy creations are excellent.

There are also classic rations to share and burgers. (www.lakazuela.com)

Satistegi SEAFOOD €€

14 MAP P78, B2

Revel in sweeping sea views and excellent seafood at this contemporary bar-restaurant in Algorta.

The blond-wood interior, with herringbone floors, high tables and black-and-white photos of

Getxo, is a relaxed spot to linger over *pintxos* from the marble bar or larger dishes, such as a platter of grilled prawns or fried calamari, and a bottle of wine. (www.facebook.com/satistegi)

Brasserie Igeretxe

BASQUE €€€

15 MAP P78, D2

Views of the beach, bay and hills beyond extend from the dining room and terrace of this fine-dining restaurant inside the landmark Hotel Igeretxe.

Baby squid cooked in its own ink, pig's trotters from Deba on the Central Basque Coast sautéed in local cider, and raspberry sponge with apple and *txakoli* sorbet are among its menu highlights. (www.brasserie-igeretxe.com; 🛜)

Drinking

Bar Arrantzale

BAR

16 MAP P78, A2

With its delightful plane tree-shaded cobbled terrace cooled by the afternoon sea breeze and its charming setting in Getxo's whitewashed Puerto Viejo, this laid-back bar is a top spot to slow down over a glass of wine or beer. Nibble on *pintxos* – the *morcillas* (blood sausages) and cod-stuffed peppers are excellent – or a ration of chorizo in cider and local Idiazabal cheese. (www.arrantzale.com)

Aixerrota Windmill

El Paladar BAR

17 MAP P78, E7

Grab a drink and take a seat on the terrace of the Gran Hotel Puente Colgante.

You'll be perfectly positioned to admire views of the famous bridge and watch the world stroll past on the waterfront promenade, while enjoying an Amer Picon Basque cocktail (bittersweet orange liqueur, grenadine, brandy and soda water). (www.puentecolgante-boutiquehotel.com)

Portu Zaharra Bar PUB

18 MAP P78, A2

Park yourself on the steps at Getxo's Puerto Viejo alongside this traditional white-and-green cottage and take in the sea views, while sampling the local tipple of choice, *txakoli,* a glass of *sagardoa* (cider), or an ice-cold Basque craft beer.

They also offer a wide range of *pintxos,* including mushroom, ham and caramelised goat's cheese. (www.portuzaharra.com)

Casa Vicente BAR

19 MAP P78, E7

Pintxo bar and nightlife spot Casa Vicente packs in the garrulous beer- and cocktail-loving crowds on weekends.

It's hidden in the old lanes just up from the seafront, and is well worth seeking out any time for its quality *pintxos,* fine drink selections (try a vermouth) and ambient tunes.

Gexto Old Port

Shopping

Ana Valladares FASHION & ACCESSORIES

20 MAP P78, F5

Renowned local fashion designer Ana Valladares creates highly distinctive, ultra-stylish women's fashion incorporating straight lines and unusual prints, as well as bags, scarves and hats, here in Getxo.

Garments can be altered in-house. (www.facebook.com/AnaValladaresQueModa)

Mika Kids Concept Store TOYS

21 MAP P78, F5

If you're shopping for kids, don't miss this sunny little shop near the bridge. You'll find quality gear, such as backpacks by Swedish label Fjallraven Kanken, and 100% natural baby toys by Oli & Carol. Lots of cuddly things and eco-friendly wooden toy sets round out the offerings. (www.mikakids-conceptstore.com)

La Granja Selección FOOD & DRINKS

22 MAP P78, F5

Founded in 1965, this much-loved deli has all the essentials for assembling a first-rate picnic: wines, cheeses, hams, olive oils, fresh breads, antipasti, chocolates, tins of smoked fish and more. (www.lagranjaseleccion.es)

Cycling in Getxo

Getxo's waterfront path is great for a spin, stretching 4km from just south of the **Puente Colgante** (p80) transporter bridge to Algorta's old port area, **Peurto Viejo** (Map p78, A2).

Hire wheels from **Bicis Txofi** (Map p78, F5), which can get you outfitted with a decent hybrid bike. Alternatively, take advantage of Getxo's inexpensive bike-sharing network, **GetxoBizi** (www.getxobizi.com). This has 13 stations scattered around the area, including one half a block north of the Puente Colgante. A day pass allows unlimited rentals in increments of one hour; you'll have to register online (it's easy), and you'll need a mobile phone with you in order to check out a bike.

Worth a Trip
Understand the Past at Gernika

A name synonymous with the brutality of the Spanish Civil War, Gernika (Spanish: Guernica) suffered a devastating bombing raid that levelled the city in 1937. That harrowing April day left a deep mark on the city's identity. Following the war, Gernika was quickly reconstructed, and today excellent museums deal with the bombing and indestructibility of Basque culture through the ages.

Gernika is an easy day trip from Bilbao by Euskotren train from Atxuri train station (€3.40, one hour). Trains run every half-hour; buses also make the journey.

Museo de la Paz de Gernika

Gernika's seminal experience is a visit to the **Gernika Peace Museum** (www.museodelapaz.org), where audiovisual displays reveal the horror of war in the Basque Country and worldwide. You'll even get to experience what it was like on that fateful day with a recreation inside a local living room. On nearby Calle Allende Salazar is a ceramic-tile version of Picasso's *Guernica*.

Museo de Euskal Herría

Housed in the beautiful 18th-century Palacio de Montefuerte, the **Museum of the Basque Country** (www.bizkaikoa.bizkaia.eus) illustrates Basque history through old maps, engravings and other documents and portraits.

Parque de los Pueblos de Europa

The city's **park** features two monumental sculptures commemorating what happened in the town, one by renowned Basque sculptor Eduardo Chillida and the other by Henry Moore. Adjacent is the **Tree of Gernika**, under which the Basque parliament met from medieval times to 1876.

Nearby: Cuevas de Santimamiñe

Located 6.5km northeast of Gernika, the walls of this **cave system** (www.santimamiñe.com) are decorated with around 50 different Neolithic paintings depicting bison, horses, rhinos and the like. To protect these delicate artworks, only reproductions are on display. Tours lasting 90 minutes take place on the hour. Call ahead to reserve an English-speaking guide.

★ Top Tips

○ The tourist information authority (turismo.gernika-lumo.eus) has an excellent audio tour you can download, taking in all the major sights, including an immersion experience inside the Refugios Antiereos Pasealeku (Civil War air raid shelters).

○ Within the 220-sq-km bird-filled Urdaibai Biosphere Reserve, the **Urdaibai Bird Center** (www.birdcenter.org) is 5.5km northeast of Gernika. Your own wheels are the easiest way to reach this sight.

✕ Take a Break

Top-notch *pintxo* bars concentrate on and around Calle Pablo Picasso; **Auzokoa** is a standout. If you're after something bigger, head to **Batzoki** (www.batzoki-gernika.business.site) for whole grilled fish and tuna-belly salad.

Explore
Central Basque Coast

The coastline between Bilbao and San Sebastián has spectacular seascapes, with cove after cove of sun-dappled waves and verdant fields suddenly ending where cliffs plunge into the sea, along with pretty beaches, scenic coastal walks and fabulous seafood.

The Short List

○ **Getaria (p92)** Exploring the grilled-fish capital of Spain, a medieval fishing village with historic streets, a fashion museum and superb seafood restaurants.

○ **San Juan de Gaztelugatxe (p95)** Making a pilgrimage to this rocky isle topped by a hermitage – one of the most photogenic sights in the Basque Country.

○ **Basque Coast Geopark (p100)** Discovering the coastline's dramatic cliffs and astonishing rock formations on foot or by boat.

○ **Isla de San Nicolás (p98)** Walking out to the island at low tide and marvelling at the coloured houses surrounding the port.

○ **Mundaka (p96)** Riding the legendary waves.

Getting There & Around

🚗 Most travellers explore by car; hire companies are located in San Sebastián and Bilbao.

🚌 Regular services run from San Sebastián via the coast to Lekeitio (€7.45, 1½ hours). Bilbao has services via Bermeo (€2.55, 50 minutes) to Mundaka (€2.55, one hour). Travelling between Mundaka and Lekeitio (€2.85, 1½ hours) requires a change inland in Gernika.

Central Basque Coast Map on p94

San Juan de Gaztelugatxe (p95) FOTOKON/SHUTTERSTOCK ©

Top Experience 📷
Discover Coastal Basque Lifestyle in Getaria

🎯 MAP P94, D3

The medieval fishing settlement of Getaria is a world away from nearby cosmopolitan San Sebastián and is a wonderful place to get a feel for coastal Basque culture. The old village tilts gently downhill to a tiny harbour and a short but very pleasant beach, almost totally sheltered from all but the heaviest Atlantic swells.

Buses run regularly from San Sebastián to Getaria (€2.75, one hour). From Bilbao, you'll need to change in Eibar and Zarautz to reach Getaria (€6.60, 2½ hours).

Cristóbal Balenciaga Museoa

Although Getaria is mainly about sun, sand and seafood, don't miss a visit to the **Cristóbal Balenciaga Museoa** (www.cristobalbalenciaga museoa.com). Local son Cristóbal became a giant in the fashion world in the 1950s and '60s, and this impressive museum showcases some of his best works. Start with a 23-minute video (English version available) that gives an overview of the fashion innovator once viewed as the king of couture. Afterwards, wander through the futuristic galleries, where artfully lit displays showcase pieces from his wide-ranging collection, including his Infanta gown, inspired by costumes worn by Spanish princesses as painted by Diego Velázquez.

Iglesia de San Salvador

With its unusual shape, sloping wooden floors, and nautical atmosphere, Getaria's striking 1397-built Gothic **church** is well worth a stop. Features worth noting include the gravestone of the great navigator Juan Sebastián Elcano, who was baptised here, and an underground passage that leads to Getaria's harbour.

El Ratón

At the end of the harbour is a forested former island known as El Ratón (the Mouse), which was attached via a breakwater in the 15th century. Perhaps it was this giant mouse that first encouraged the town's most famous son, the sailor Juan Sebastián Elcano, to take to the ocean. In the early 16th century, he became the first person to complete a circumnavigation of the globe, after Magellan, the captain of his ship, died halfway through the endeavour.

★ Top Tips

o Dining is a big part of the Getaria experience. Be sure to reserve ahead, even at lunchtime.

o Produced by vineyards on the surrounding hillsides, *txakoli* pairs perfectly with seafood.

o Walk to Zarautz (p101) by the coast along part of the Camino del Norte, which goes all the way to Santiago de Compostela.

✕ Take a Break

Watch your fish being grilled outdoors while looking out across the ocean at the excellent **Kaia Kaipe** (www.kaia-kaipe.com).

Dine on catches landed in front of **Txoko Getaria** (www.txokogetaria.com).

For slightly more affordable options, head up the main street to **Restaurante Politena** (www.politenagetaria.com), which also offers tasty seafood straight from the grill, and grilled Navarran asparagus for vegetarians.

Bermeo

1 MAP P94, B2

This fishing port 35km northeast of Bilbao is very popular with locals making weekend day trips. There's much history hidden in its laneways, as some centuries ago Bermeo was a centre of the whaling industry. Scenic outlooks offer memorable views over the rugged seashore, although the only beaches in the area are rocky and wave-battered.

One of the most photographed features of the Basque coast, 10km to Bermeo's northwest, is the small, rocky isle of **San Juan de Gaztelugatxe** (www.tiketa.eus/gaztelugatxe). Accessed from the mainland by climbing 241 steps via a stone footbridge, it's topped by a hermitage, Ermita de San Juan de Gaztelugatxe, which was built by the Knights Templar in the 10th century. Because of its insane popularity, which soared after it became the setting for Dragonstone in *Game of Thrones* season seven, it's necessary to reserve online in advance at tiketa.eus/gaztelugatxe. Local tradition says that it was named after St John the Baptist, who allegedly visited the island.

Small but absorbing, Bermeo's **Arrantzaleen Museoa** (www.bizkaikoa.bizkaia.eus) has model ships, shipbuilding tools and implements such as harpoons that provide an overview of the history of Basque fishing. It spans the lives, work and customs of fishers, and the boats

San Juan de Gaztelugatxe

Underwater Winery

The world's first underwater winery, **Crusoe Treasure** (www.underwaterwine.com), ages its vintages 20m below the surface on an artificial reef. Tastings of its whites and reds are available on land at its tasting room. For a truly immersive experience, take a scenic boat ride out to the reef, where barnacle-encrusted bottles are hauled up for you to taste. Swimming off the boat is possible; prices also include *pintxos*.

and techniques used throughout the centuries, as well as a small section covering the Basque naval forces. It's located in the 15th-century **Torre de Ercilla**; displays also cover the history of the tower itself. Signage is in Basque and Spanish; an English-language leaflet is available.

Dine on seafood classics at the excellent **Batun-Batun Taberna** (Calle Istua 2) while looking out across the colourful port. It serves mouth-watering plates of grilled scallops, tasty tuna belly, and crispy shrimp tortillas.

Hegaluze (www.hegaluze.com) offers scenic boat tours from Bermeo harbour either towards Elantxobe or the other way to San Juan de Gaztelugatxe (€13).

Mundaka

2 MAP P94, B2

Home to one of the best left-hand waves in Europe, with 200m-plus rides and deep barrels, Mundaka is a name of legend for surfers across the world. Mundaka is also a resolutely Basque port with a pretty main square and harbour area.

From March to October, **Mundaka Surf Shop** (www.mundakasurfshop.com) runs a reputable surf school, and leads guided one-hour SUP board tours along the river (€40). You can hire gear year-round, including surf and SUP boards, kayaks, bodyboards and wetsuits. Lessons take place on scenic beach **Playa de Laida** on the eastern side of the estuary (a 23km drive or a mere 200m-or-so paddle from Mundaka).

Elantxobe

3 MAP P94, C2

Located 14km west of Lekeitio, the tiny hamlet of Elantxobe, with its ice-cream-coloured houses clasping like geckos to an almost sheer cliff face, is a pretty spot. There's no beach here, but it's a cute village to explore, and on hot days you can join the local children jumping into the sea from the harbour walls. Take care on the walk, as it's a very steep descent from the main road to the waterfront.

Ea

4 MAP P94, C2

Water surrounds the photogenic little village of Ea, 10km west of Lekeitio. Sitting at the head of a narrow estuary, the colourful lanes of the 16th-century village are linked by humpbacked medieval bridges. At the seaward end of the village is a sandy patch of beach.

Ea is the starting point for several scenic walks in the area, ranging from 5km to 7km. Among the most scenic is the 5km **Sendero de las Letanías**. This well-marked path begins near the church and heads up to Bedarona for marvellous views, before descending towards the rugged coastline and looping back to Ea. Stop by the seasonal **tourist office** (www.eaturismo.com) for a map and trail info. When it's closed, pick up maps at tourist offices in Bilbao, Getaria or San Sebastián.

Right opposite the bus stop in Ea is lively **Txangurru** (www.facebook.com/txangurrutaberna), a traditional Basque tavern and a popular spot for a drink and simple yet tasty *pintxos* such as tuna with caramelised onion and ham with Gernika peppers.

Lekeitio

5 MAP P94, C2

Bustling Lekeitio is gorgeous. The attractive old core is centred on the **Basílica de la Asunción de Santa María** (www.basilicadelekeitio.com). This grand late-Gothic

Mundaka

Basque Sports

The national sport of the Basque country is *pelota basque* (aka jai alai), and every village in the region has its own *fronton* (court) – often backing up against the village church. Pelota can be played in several different ways: bare-handed, with small wooden rackets, or with a long hand-basket called a *chistera,* with which the player can throw the ball at speeds of up to 300km/h. It's possible to see pelota matches throughout the region during summer. One place where you can get a primer is **Miruaitz Taberna**, next to the village *fronton* in Mutriku. Juanjo, a player in the former US pro teams, now coaches the next generation while his wife Caterina runs the cafe. Games take place on Fridays from around 7pm, except during August.

Basque sports aren't just limited to pelota: there's also log cutting, stone lifting, bale tossing and tug of war. Most stem from the day-to-day activities of the region's farmers and fisherfolk, and are kept alive at numerous fiestas.

---

church, complete with flying buttresses topped with pinnacles, offers a vision of grandeur surprising for such a small town. In fact, Lekeitio's prolific whaling industry helped fund such extravagance. Highlights include the frieze-covered west facade and a Gothic-Flemish altarpiece that's the third-largest in Spain after Seville and Toledo.

Lekeitio's busy harbour is lined by multicoloured, half-timbered old buildings – some of which house fine seafood restaurants and *pintxo* bars, but for most visitors, it's the beaches that are the main draw.

When you're feeling peckish, stop off at **Kaia**, a cosy tavern with a good array of *pintxos* and homemade *tortilla* (Spanish omelette). They also do an excellent breakfast selection of topped toasts, fresh juices and pastries.

One of the great attractions of Lekeitio is the rocky island of **Isla de San Nicolás**, known in Basque as Garraitz, sitting just offshore of the main beach (Playa Isuntza). When the tides are low, a paved path littered with crabs (very slippery) appears, allowing visitors to stroll straight out to the island, and take a 200m trail to the top for a fine view over the seaside. Be mindful of the tides, so you don't have to swim back! The **tourist office** (www.lekeitioturismo.eus) posts tidal charts.

Situated 800m south of the centre, **Mesón Arropain** serves some of the best seafood for miles around. The chef lets the high-quality ingredients speak for themselves in simple but beautifully prepared dishes. Start off with its famous *arrain zopa* (fish soup) and move on to *zapo beltza* (deep-sea anglerfish with fried Gernika peppers) or *legatzen kokotxak* (hake with prawns and clams). There's an excellent wine selection.

Mutriku

6 MAP P94, D3

A fishing town through and through, Mutriku, which dates from the early 13th century, is tightly wedged between slices of steep hills. It's an attractive village of tall houses painted in blues and greens, and steps that tumble steeply downwards to the port. There's a small beach on the outskirts with two natural sea pools, a major draw on hot sunny days. Scenic trails go 4.5km west to Saturraran and 15km east through the Basque Coast Geopark (p100) via the beachside village of Deba all the way to Zumaia.

Zumaia

7 MAP P94, D3

Where the Urola and Narrondo rivers converge, the industrial port town of Zumaia has a charming centre and two popular beaches located along the world's longest stretch of flysch sedimentary rock strata. On the town's western side, **Playa de Izturun** is wedged in among cliffs where fossils in the rock include ammonites. On the eastern side of the estuary, 2.5km

Mutriku

east of Playa de Izturun, is a more traditional stretch of sand, **Playa de Santiago**. The village is also a gateway to the wondrous cliffs of the Basque Coast Geopark (p100), a geological wonder spanning 60 million years.

Zarautz

8 ⊙ MAP P94, D3

Zarautz consists of a 2.5km-long soft sand beach (the Basque Country's longest) backed by

Geological Marvels of the Central Coast

Between the Bay of Biscay and the western Pyrenees lies an extraordinary geological treasure, a series of rock layers, built up over time, that offer an astonishing survey of more than 60 million years of life on earth. Running for 13km along the coast, these natural formations known as flysch deposits give a geological record from 50 to 110 million years ago and were formed following the collision of Iberia – once an island – with the continent of Europe. Some geologists believe that a thin black layer embedded in the rocks occurred around 65 million years ago and indicates when an asteroid struck the earth and caused the mass extinction of dinosaurs.

The site, comprising some 89 sq km, is protected as the **Basque Coast Geopark** (www.geoparkea.com), and was designated a Unesco Global Geopark in 2015. It spreads across the municipalities of Zumaia, Mutriku and Deba, with marked pathways travelling over the site, though sites of particular geological interest can also be visited on **boat trips** (www.geoparkea.com/en/guided-tours) departing from Zumaia.

The other great geological attraction of the region is karst, formations made by the eroded limestone of an ancient tropical sea. This slow-acting erosion led to the creation of caves, used by some of the region's earliest humans as places of refuge when the planet turned cold. Their imaginative paintings are preserved in places such as Ekainberri, home to some 70 paintings dating back around 14,000 years – and yet another Unesco World Heritage Site.

The park is set amid the hilly countryside of the interior, which is today rich Basque farmland. It is bounded to the south by a group of mountains made of Urgonian limestone, which were once barrier reefs. This unusual landscape formed by tectonic deformations is full of paleontological evidence of its marine past, with fossils of bivalves, calcareous plankton and ammonites from the Cretaceous period. Deba and Mutriku are blessed with important archaeological sites, still being studied today.

a largely modern strip of tower blocks.

The beach has some of the best surfing in the area and there are a number of surf schools, including **Moor Surf Eskola** (www.moorsurfeskola.com).

On the promenade overlooking the beach, they run a variety of lessons for all levels of ability overseen by professional instructors and also hire out boards and wetsuits.

It's well worth detouring from the sands to explore the tangle of medieval streets.

On one of its liveliest little lanes, Zarautz's 1903-opened **market** is a culinary treasure-chest of great produce from the Basque region.

You'll find excellent seasonal fruit and vegetables, breads, delectable cheeses, glistening olives, cured hams and sausages, seafood, wines, ciders and other enticements.

Okamika (www.okamika.es) is a jewel-box-sized wine and *pintxo* bar, with exposed stone and whitewashed walls.

Stop in for smoked sardines, grilled foie gras with fig jam or grilled scallops with sea urchin roe, matched with a changing selection of by-the-glass wines and over 40 different gins.

Zarautz' **Photomuseum** (www.photomuseum.name) explores the development of photography and moving pictures.

Basque Coast Geopark

Start up on the 4th floor and work your way downstairs, taking in displays on ombrascopes, magic lanterns and the early cinematic creations of the Lumière brothers. The 2nd and 1st floors are devoted to photography.

Don't miss the early 20th-century photographs of the Bilbao artist Luis de Ocharan, who captured fascinating vignettes of Basque rural and urban life in his grainy images.

Need a break? Stop off at cute little **Pastelería Aizpurua** (www.pasteleria-aizpurua.negocio.site) for a filled bagel, a slice of fruity tart, or a warming coffee.

San Sebastián Neighbourhoods

Hondarribia & Pasaia (p149)
Enjoy superb seafood, stunning sea views, maritime history and verdant peaks in historic Hondarribia and the old port of Pasaia.

San Sebastián Parte Vieja (p105)
This nest of old streets contains the finest *pintxo* bars in Spain. The aquarium, churches and museum will also appeal.

San Sebastián Gros (p141)
Hang on the beach with the surfers, admire the modern architecture of the Kursaal and devote yourself to discovering new culinary horizons.

San Sebastián New Town & Monte Igueldo (p123)
Grandiose and elegant, San Sebastián's new town is perfect for wandering, shopping and enjoying the funfair at Monte Igueldo.

Central Basque Coast (p91)
Pretty villages and a dramatic coast make this a scenic destination for a road trip. After a seafood meal, bask on a golden beach.

- Getaria
- Aquarium
- Monte Igueldo
- San Telmo Museoa
- Playa de la Concha
- Chillida Leku

Explore
San Sebastián

From its delightful Old Town, fascinating museums and fantastic pintxos restaurants, there are a multitude of reasons why San Sebastián is a tourist favourite. This gorgeous town also has some of Europe's most famous surf beaches on its doorstep.

San Sebastián Parte Vieja **105**

**San Sebastián New Town
& Monte Igueldo** **123**

San Sebastián Gros **141**

Hondarribia & Pasaia **149**

San Sebastián's Walking Tours

Following the Pintxo Trail 110
Old & New in San Sebastián 128
St-Jean de Luz, France 156

Explore
San Sebastián Parte Vieja

It only takes a few minutes to stroll the length of San Sebastián's Parte Vieja (Old Town), but it might take half a lifetime to sample all the temptations. Every other building seems to house a bar or restaurant, each of which is in intense competition with the others to please the palate.

The Short List

- **San Telmo Museoa (p106)** Learning about Basque history at this captivating museum partially set inside a 16th-century convent.

- **Monte Urgull (p113)** Walking up this verdant hill for spectacular beach and city views from the old ramparts.

- **Aquarium (p108)** Watching mighty sea creatures glide along inside this excellent aquarium's massive tunnel.

- **Basílica de Santa María del Coro (p113)** Admiring the elaborate facade and altarpiece of San Sebastián's 18th-century baroque beauty.

- **Isla de Santa Clara (p115)** Catching a boat out to this pretty offshore island in La Concha Bay.

Getting There & Around

🚶 San Sebastián is small, and with the Parte Vieja sitting pretty much at the centre, it's almost always easier and quicker to walk here from elsewhere.

🚌 Buses linking to other parts of San Sebastián use the bus stops on Alameda del Boulevard.

San Sebastián Parte Vieja Map on p112

Parte Vieja MARCHELLO74/SHUTTERSTOCK ©

Top Experience 📷
Delve into Basque Culture and Society at San Telmo Museoa

Although it's one of the newer museums in the Basque Country, the San Telmo Museoa has actually been around since the 1920s, occupying a 16th-century Dominican convent. After a refurbishment, the enlarged space now hosts an array of fascinating displays, including historical artefacts, 20th-century social history and artwork, with a focus on Basque culture and society.

🎯 MAP P112, D2

www.santelmomuseoa.eus

The Design

The Basque Country likes to provide its collections with eye-catching homes and the San Telmo Museoa is no exception. The museum has taken a 16th-century Dominican convent with a beautiful cloister and added memorable contemporary architecture, including a vertical garden.

Sert Canvases

One of the museum's proudest possessions are the Sert Canvases, located inside the church. The work, created in 1929 by José María Sert, illustrates some of the most important events in San Sebastián's history, including panels on shipbuilding and the sacred oak tree of Gernika.

Memory Traces

Covering the vast period from prehistory to the 19th century, the Memory Traces exhibition delves into Basque origins and the moment in which Basques first looked out to the wider world and set off by boat to explore it.

Awakening of Modernity

This exhibition covers the great transformations in Basque society that took place during the 19th and 20th centuries, when lifestyles changed from rural to industrial and urban. Exhibits range from traditional farming equipment to 1960s pop culture.

Temporary Exhibitions

The museum prides itself on the broad outlook of its collection, but it's in the frequently changing temporary exhibitions that its diversity becomes truly apparent. These exhibitions might focus for a few months on the collateral damage of war and the ill treatment of refugees; next it could be all about Basque sports and mountaineering.

★ Top Tips

- Labelling is in Spanish, Basque and occasionally English, with free audio guides available in other languages.

- The connection between pieces can be vague – get an audio guide to make things clearer.

- The museum is closed on Mondays.

- Entry is free on Tuesdays.

✕ Take a Break

San Telmo Museoa has an in-house restaurant **Zazpi STM** (www.zazpistm.com).

Almost next door to the museum, La Cuchara de San Telmo (p111) serves some of the best *pintxos* in San Sebastián's old town.

Top Experience
Enter an Aquatic Wonderland at Aquarium

Brace yourself as huge sharks approach the thick glass panes, and marvel at otherworldly jellyfish. Highlights of this excellent aquarium include the deep-ocean and coral-reef exhibits, a 12m-long skeleton of an endangered North Atlantic right whale, and the long tunnel through the main tank, where creatures of the deep swim all around you. Also here is a maritime museum section.

 MAP P112, A3

www.aquariumss.com

Oceanarium & Tunnel

The aquarium's biggest draw for young and old alike is the giant oceanarium tank. It includes a see-through tunnel, where you'll see razor-toothed grey nurse (aka sand tiger) sharks, graceful rays, cute turtles, moray eels and various other denizens of the deep. Shark feedings take place at noon on Tuesdays, Thursdays and Saturdays.

Tactile Tank

A favourite with children is the tactile tank, where they can wet their finger tips as they try to handle sea urchins, starfish, blennies, prawns and more. Towards the end of the aquarium is a tank containing slightly transparent shark eggs (dogfish, not great whites) that allow you to see the unborn sharks wriggling about.

Coral Reefs & Mangrove Swamps

Everyone enjoys the oversized tanks of beautiful corals and butterfly-bright tropical marine fish. The 18m-long mangrove swamp display with tree roots reaching into the depths reveals some of the unusual creatures that live in this unique environment.

Maritime Exhibition

Although you'll arrive expecting frenzies of fish in big glass tanks, the first exhibition at the Aquarium explores the region's colourful maritime and natural history. From whale skeletons to model ships, the journey takes to the high seas, exploring the Basques' long and adventurous seafaring past, revealing how they were accomplished whalers and in-demand navigators.

★ Top Tips

- Allow at least 1½ hours for a visit.
- Last tickets are sold one hour before closing.
- For a truly unique (pricey) experience, an aquarium sleepover package is available.
- Audio guides (€2) are worth hiring for more in-depth information.

✕ Take a Break

There's no cafe within the aquarium but the surrounding port has a number of decent seafood restaurants, including Kofradia (p117).

Perched above the aquarium (and accessed by a lift) is **Bokado Mikel Santamaría** (www.bokadomikelsantamaria.com)

Walking Tour

Following the Pintxo Trail

There's nothing the people of San Sebastián enjoy more than strolling from bar to bar with friends, sampling one pintxo after another. This walk takes in a selection of the best places to try delicious morsels along with a glass of wine or beer in the atmospheric laneways of the Parte Vieja.

Walk Facts

Start La Mejíllonera
Finish Bar Sport
Length 625m; three hours

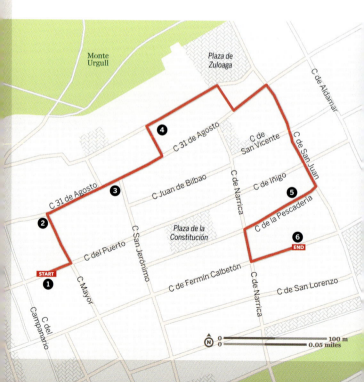

❶ La Mejíllonera

Come to **La Mejíllonera** to discover mussels in various glorious forms – including in spicy tomato sauce, with a vinaigrette, in a wine sauce or simply steamed but utterly delectable. All go down nicely with *patatas bravas* (fried potatoes) and an ice-cold beer.

❷ Casa Vergara

Casa Vergara (https://grupogarrancho.com/carta/casa-vergara) is a bustling *pintxos* spot where the bar is piled high with food, including some decent vegetarian options. Each one is labelled in Spanish, Basque and English so you've a better idea of what you're getting, perfect for this early stage of your walk. They serve a decent *txakoli* (white wine) and there's also an oyster bar for something a little more decadent.

❸ Gandarias

An obligatory destination for anyone interested in San Sebastián's foodie hot spots, **Gandarias** (www.restaurantegandarias.com) has a sterling reputation for its artfully prepared *pintxos*. You'll find all the classics on hand, with house specials such as seared foie gras with redcurrants, Joselito Iberian ham, scrumptious *solomillo* (tenderloin) sandwiches, stuffed mushrooms and delicious crab pie.

❹ La Cuchara de San Telmo

The supremely creative kitchen at **La Cuchara de San Telmo** offers miniature *nueva cocina vasca* (Basque nouvelle cuisine). Unlike many San Sebastián bars, this one doesn't have any *pintxos* laid out on the bar top; instead you must order from the blackboard menu behind the counter. Order delights include slow-roasted suckling pig and veal cheeks in red wine.

❺ Bar Nestor

Wonderfully eccentric **Bar Nestor** (www.facebook.com/BarNestorSS) has a cult following for its friendly staff, its tortillas made with green peppers (just one style of tortilla is cooked at lunch and at dinner), and its steaks.

❻ Bar Sport

It's usually standing-room-only at **Bar Sport**. People flock to this *pintxos* place with the misleading name for its uniquely Basque bites, including the *crema de erizo* (sea urchin) and the *txangurro crepe* (spider crab pancake).

San Sebastián Parte Vieja

For reviews see
- Top Experiences p106
- Sights p113
- Eating p116
- Drinking p119
- Entertainment p120
- Shopping p120

Sights

Basílica de
Santa María del Coro BASILICA

1 MAP P112, D3

The Parte Vieja's most photogenic building is this baroque basilica, completed in 1774. Its ornate facade depicts St Sebastian and the altarpiece is dedicated to San Sebastián's other patron saint, Our Lady of the Choir.

Monte Urgull MOUNTAIN

2 MAP P112, B2

You can walk to the summit of Monte Urgull (123m), topped by the low castle walls of the Castillo de la Mota and a grand statue of Christ, by taking a path from Plaza de Zuloaga, the steps behind Basílica de Santa María del Coro or from the aquarium. The views are breathtaking and the shady woodland on the way up is a peaceful retreat from the city.

Castillo de la Mota CASTLE

3 MAP P112, C2

At the summit of Monte Urgull, this stone fortress is but the latest incarnation of many fortifications that have existed here since the 12th century. It's well worth huffing your way to the top for the impressive views and the intriguing exhibitions of the Casa de la Historia (p114), located inside the castle walls.

Monte Urgull

Iglesia de San Vicente

Casa de la Historia — MUSEUM

4 MAP P112, B2

Inside the grounds of the Castillo de la Mota (p113) is this small museum focusing on the city's history. It has audiovisual exhibits that touch on San Sebastián's traditional festivals, historical artefacts from days past (including military uniforms used in the Carlist Wars), and photographs and models showing the city's evolution over the years. Views from the rooftop are exceptional. (www.santelmomuseoa.eus)

Museo Marítimo Vasco — MUSEUM

5 MAP P112, B3

This excellent little museum is one of the few in the Basque Country to offer a frank, revisionist appraisal of the region's seafaring and naval history. There is no permanent collection, just long-term exhibitions, which in the past have featured thoughtful takes on themes such as shipwrecks, women and the sea, and the Basque role in whaling and slavery. Signage is usually in English, Spanish, Basque and French. (www.itsasmuseoa.eus)

Construcción Vacía — SCULPTURE

6 MAP P112, A2

At the base of Monte Urgull is Jorge Oteiza's *Construcción Vacía (Empty Space)* sculpture. Oteiza (1908–2003) was a renowned painter, sculptor and writer who was born and brought up close to San Sebastián. An award winner at the 1957 São Paulo Biennale, the rust-red work looks best on a dark and stormy day or at sunset.

Iglesia de San Vicente — CHURCH

7 MAP P112, E2

Lording it over the Parte Vieja, this striking church is thought to be the oldest building in San Sebastián. Its origins date to the late 12th century, but it was rebuilt in its current Gothic form in the early 1500s. The towering facade gives onto an echoing vaulted interior, featuring an elaborate gold altarpiece and a 19th-century French organ. Also impressive are the stained-glass rose windows. (www.san-vicente-parroquia.es)

Plaza de la Constitución SQUARE

8 MAP P112, D3

One of the Basque Country's most attractive city squares, the Plaza de la Constitución was built in 1813 at the heart of the old town on the site of an older square. It was once used as a bullring; the balconies of the fringing houses were rented to spectators.

Isla de Santa Clara ISLAND

9 MAP P112, A4

Lying 750m offshore from Playa de la Concha, this little island is accessible by **Motoras de la Isla** (www.motorasdelaisla.com) boats that run every half-hour from the fishing port in the summer.

At low tide the island gains its own tiny beach and you can climb its forested paths to a small lighthouse.

There are also picnic tables and a summertime kiosk.

Darwin Rentals WATER SPORTS

10 MAP P112, C3

On the harbourfront, Darwin Rentals hires out state-of-the-art inflatable two-person kayaks, regular kayaks and SUPs (stand-up paddleboards), as well as bikes, electric scooters and motorised skateboards.

Friendly staff provide great insider tips on the best locations to use the equipment. (www.darwin-rentals.es)

Plaza de la Constitución

Post-Lunch Planning

Make sure you have a plan for after-lunch activities, as most shops close for a long siesta. It's a perfect time to head to one of the bigger museums, or the beach for a bit of seaside relaxation.

Eating

Bodegón Alejandro BASQUE €€€

11 MAP P112, E3

Tucked down the steps off a pedestrian-packed street, this handsome cellar restaurant is acclaimed for its Basque cooking. The small, changing menu has succulent treats such as local Idiazabal cheese soufflé, spider-crab salad with fennel cream, crispy-skin hake with a zesty lemon vinaigrette, and stewed quail rice. (www.bodegonalejandro.com)

Casa Urola PINTXOS €

12 MAP P112, E3

Founded in 1956, Casa Urola has hefty stone walls, hams hanging above the bar and a blackboard menu chalking up the day's *pintxos*. Join the lunch and evening crowds flocking for perfectly turned-out bites, such as grilled white asparagus, foie gras with pear compote, hake tacos, and mushroom and Idiazabal cheese tart. (www.casaurolajatetxea.es)

Restaurante Kokotxa GASTRONOMY €€€

13 MAP P112, C3

Hidden in an overlooked Parte Vieja alley, this Michelin-starred restaurant rewards those who search. Most people opt for the *menú de mercado* and enjoy the flavours of the busy city market. Note that there are just 30 seats, making advance reservations essential, and that no-choice menus mean dietary restrictions can't be accommodated. (www.restaurante-kokotxa.com)

Bar Borda Berri PINTXOS €€

14 MAP P112, E3

Perennially popular Bar Borda Berri is an old-school *pintxo* bar – with black-and-white chequerboard floors and mustard-coloured walls hung with old photos and strands of garlic – that really lives up to the hype. Hungry diners crowd in for house specials such as braised veal cheeks in wine, mushroom and Idiazabal sheep's cheese risotto, and beef-rib skewers.

Txepetxa PINTXOS €

15 MAP P112, E3

The humble *antxoa* (anchovy) is elevated to royal status at this old-fashioned, wood-panelled local favourite. You can order it in over a dozen different ways, topped with everything from salmon roe to spider-crab mayonnaise. (www.facebook.com/bartxepetxa)

Txuleta

PINTXOS €€

16 MAP P112, D3

A *txuleta* is a cut of beef and this is the place to sample some wonderful melt-in-your mouth examples – try the *pintxo txuleta*, a mini-kebab of three bite-sized chunks of tender beef, or *solomillo al Oporto* (crusty bread topped with sirloin with port sauce). Its restaurant serves a full menu of steaks as well as seafood. (www.txuletarestaurante.com)

Restaurante Muxumartin

BASQUE €€

17 MAP P112, D3

A plucky newcomer among more time-tested neighbours, Muxumartin focusses on substance first, then adds the style, with some of the city's most unusual *pintxos*.
 Take the locally sourced *zamburiñas* (scallops) for example, served with green curry and wakame seaweed, or the grilled squid with smoked eel dashi and inked onions. (https://muxumartin.com)

Astelena

BASQUE €€€

18 MAP P112, F3

With a whitewashed main dining room and stone-walled cellar, this is a classy place to linger over beautifully prepared seafood and roast meat dishes. Highlights include chargrilled squid with caramelised onions, smoked duck breast with burnt-orange marmalade, and rice with octopus and clams. (www.restauranteastelena.com)

Kofradia

SEAFOOD €€

19 MAP P112, C3

Kofradia is best known for its top-quality tuna (a type known as *bonito*) dishes, including as a burger and a tuna steak marinated with almonds. Only fish caught by local fleets in the nearby Cantabrian Sea using sustainable nets and lines. (https://kofradia.eus)

Dark Memories of The Duke's Visit

You might think that Calle 31 de Agosto, at the northern end of the Parte Vieja, is named after the glorious days of late summer. But not quite. The road name actually commemorates one of the darker days in San Sebastián's history. On 31 August 1813, the Duke of Wellington's Anglo-Portuguese army captured the city from the French during the Napoleonic Wars, ransacked it and then burnt it down. Only a handful of houses and the churches of **San Vicente** (p114) and the **Basílica de Santa María del Coro** (p113) survived. To make matters worse, the Spanish and British were supposed to be on the same side. Today, candles are lit on the balconies lining this street every 31 August to recall the dreadful day.

Drinking

Côte Bar   COCKTAIL BAR

20 MAP P112, D3

Once the *pintxo* bars have battened down the hatches for the night, search out this low-key cocktail bar to see in the small hours. It's a stylish place, with a black granite bar and red, orange and yellow lighting, where you can sip on classic cocktails and superlative G&Ts. (☎)

The Rise of San Sebastián

It was a queen with bad skin who first put San Sebastián on the international tourist map. In 1845, Queen Isabel II, who suffered from a skin allergy, was advised by her doctor to start bathing in the waters of the southern Bay of Biscay, which have long been known for their therapeutic properties. Her presence each summer attracted the rest of the royal court as well as plenty of aristocrats.

Belle Époque Expansion

The town's increasing popularity brought wealth and development. In 1864 the old city walls were demolished and the new city (Centro Romántico) came into being. During the early part of the 20th century, San Sebastián reached the pinnacle of its fame when Queen Maria Cristina and her court spent the summers here in the **Palacio Miramar** (p133). It was during this period that the city was given its superb belle époque makeover, which has left it with a legacy of elegant art-nouveau buildings and beachfront swagger. Even WWI couldn't put a damper on the party – the city was used by the European elite as a retreat from the war raging elsewhere.

Re-Emergence

The good times didn't last, however. The combined effects of the Spanish Civil War followed by WWII finally put out the lights, and for decades the city languished until the tide again turned in San Sebastián's favour.

In the latter half of the 20th century, the city underwent a major revival. Its overall style and excitement give it a growing reputation as an important venue for international cultural and commercial events. The beachfront area now contains some of the most expensive properties in Spain and the city is firmly entrenched on the Spanish tourist trail, which gives it a highly international feel. In 2016, it was designated European Capital of Culture, a title it shared with the Polish city of Wrocław.

Garua
CRAFT BEER

21 MAP P112, E3

Fitted out with timber panels and exposed brick, this tri-level bar has seven Basque craft beers on the taps at any one time.

Breweries represented include San Sebastián's Basqueland and Bilbao's Bidassoa; there are also bottled Basque, Spanish and international craft beers, *txakoli*, Basque spirits and liqueurs.

Be Club
CLUB

22 MAP P112, F3

Hosting DJs throughout the week and live gigs ranging from soul and funk to Afrobeat, hip-hop and acid jazz most weekends, this cool little late-night club has an extensive gin collection, craft beers and seasonally inspired cocktails. (www.beclubss.com)

Hole Pub
BAR

23 MAP P112, E3

Old-school rock music and darts are the defining features of this underground bar in the centre of Parte Vieja, which is extremely popular with locals.

There's a good cocktail list, including the bar's signature 'the Hole', made with *patxaran* (a Basque liqueur), whisky and absinthe. (www.facebook.com/theholepub)

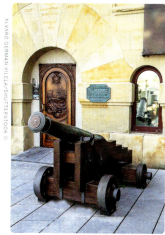

Entrance to the Aquarium (p108)

Arkaitzpe
BAR

24 MAP P112, D3

DJs spin funk and Latino beats most nights (nightly in summer) in this old-town bar's basement.

Cocktails inspired by Latin America (mojitos, caipirinhas, pisco sours, daiquiris et al) pack a punch; it also has strong sangria. Arrive early in summer, when queues form outside the door.

Entertainment

Teatro Principal
THEATRE

25 MAP P112, D4

San Sebastián's oldest theatre dates back to 1843, although it has been reconstructed over the years.

Today, the 576-seat hall hosts a packed calendar of theatre and dance performances. (www.donostiakultura.eus)

Altxerri Jazz Bar

LIVE MUSIC

26 MAP P112, F3

This jazz-and-blues temple has regular live gigs by local and international artists.

Arrive early to get a seat and enjoy a cocktail while you wait; music generally starts around 8.30pm to 9pm.

Jam sessions take over on nights with no gig; there's also an in-house art gallery that fosters the work of young contemporary artists. (https://altxerrijazzbar.com)

Etxekalte

JAZZ

27 MAP P112, C3

Near the harbour, this late-night haunt set over two floors hosts live jazz and blues, plus other genres such as traditional Basque music, and often has DJs.

Shopping

Casa Ponsol

HATS

28 MAP P112, E3

In business since 1838, this hat shop evokes the elegance of a bygone era.

The bright and sunny interior has lots of great styles for men and women with international brands such as Stetson, Kangol and Crambes, as well as authentic

Isla de Santa Clara (p115)

Panama hats and Casa Ponsol's own berets. (www.casaponsol.com)

Mercado de la Bretxa — MARKET

29 MAP P112, E3

Dating to 1870, San Sebastián's Mercado de la Bretxa is now home to chain stores, but adjacent to it, accessed via escalators in a glass kiosk-like building, is the underground covered market where every chef in the old town comes to get the freshest produce. It's an ideal place to stock up on picnic supplies.

Alboka Artesanía — ARTS & CRAFTS

30 MAP P112, E3

Crafts and objects made in the Basque Country fill this shop on one of the old town's prettiest plazas. You'll find ceramics, tea towels, marionettes, picture frames, T-shirts, pelota balls and of course those iconic oversized berets. (https://albokaartesania.com)

Beltza — MUSIC

31 MAP P112, E3

Browse for vinyl and CDs from the Basque Country and beyond at this chequerboard-tiled record shop. Cash only. (www.beltzarecords.com)

Surfing Icon

Pukas (Map p112, D4; www.pukassurf.com) is a historic name in San Sebastián's surfing circles, running a surf school near Gros' Zurriola beach and a number of shops across town, including this one in the Parte Vieja. As well as an array of boards, you can browse the full range of beach fashions, from bikinis and sunglasses to trainers, caps and T-shirts.

Aitor Lasa — FOOD & DRINKS

32 MAP P112, F3

This high-quality deli is the place to stock up on ingredients for a gourmet picnic, with a heavenly array of cheeses, mushrooms and seasonal fruit and vegetables. (www.aitorlasa.com)

Room 278 — GIFTS & SOUVENIRS

33 MAP P112, C3

Though small in size, Room 278 has loads of great gift ideas, including prints of picturesque San Sebastián scenes, rugged canvas bags, mugs, pillowcases, cushions, tea towels and more. (www.room278shop.com)

Explore
San Sebastián New Town & Monte Igueldo

A scenic area for strolling, San Sebastián's elegant new town, or Centro Romántico, has wide, straight streets lined by stately belle époque buildings and glamorous boutiques. Further west is the upmarket seaside neighbourhood of Ondarreta and fun-filled Monte Igueldo.

The Short List

- **Playa de la Concha (p124)** Lazing away the day at this lovely protected beach.

- **Monte Igueldo (p126)** Riding the funicular railway up to the funfair-topped hill with magnificent views over the seaside city.

- **Catedral del Buen Pastor de San Sebastián (p133)** Visiting the new town's soaring 19th-century cathedral.

- **Teatro Victoria Eugenia (p138)** Taking in a performance at the city's beautiful belle époque theatre.

- **Jardines de Miramar (p132)** Strolling through the grounds of a queen's former palace.

Getting There & Around

🚶 The best way to explore is on foot. From the heart of Parte Vieja it's about a 15-minute walk to Playa de la Concha's centre.

🚌 Bus 16 travels from the centre to the base of Monte Igueldo via Playa de la Concha.

San Sebastián New Town Map on p130

Playa de la Concha (p124) ALEXANDER DEMYANENKO/SHUTTERSTOCK ©

Top Experience 📷
Hit the Beach at Playa de la Concha

  MAP P130, E4

Fulfilling almost every idea of what a perfect city beach should be like, Playa de la Concha is framed by the Parte Vieja, beautiful parks and flowery belle époque buildings. Tanned and toned bodies spread across the sand throughout the long summer months, when a fiesta atmosphere prevails. Its sheltered position means the swimming is almost always safe.

The Beach

Playa de la Concha is a wide half-moon-shaped bay of soft sand, lapping waves, stunning views and a buzzing beach scene.

Tides vary enormously here; when it's high, the beach's width can be as little as 40m, so make sure your possessions don't get washed away.

Paseo de la Concha

The promenade that curves along the 1.3km-long beach, Paseo de la Concha, makes for a lovely stroll. Lined by an ornamental wrought iron balustrade, it's a favourite with joggers, cyclists and strollers, particularly in the early evening when everyone turns out to enjoy the bracing sea air and soft summer light. After dark, it's illuminated by belle époque lampposts, with magical views of the city's twinkling lights reflecting in the lapping water.

Historic Buildings

Overlooking the west of the beach, the Palacio Miramar (p133) was the summer villa of Maria Cristina, a beach-loving 19th-century royal. Further around, La Perla spa and restaurant complex is a local landmark, an ornate 1912 pavilion that was once the royal bathing house. Its saltwater spas can now be enjoyed by everyone at La Perla Thalasso Sports Centre (p134).

Beachfront Partying

The Playa is home to a number of cafes and nightlife hotspots, such as Café de la Concha (p134). For late-night dancing, the historic Bataplan Disco (p135) overlooking the sand remains the place to go.

★ Top Tips

○ The swim out to Isla de Santa Clara (p115) is tempting, but it's further than it looks. Paddle from Playa de Ondarreta (p132) instead: it's closer (about 450m) and there are summertime rest platforms on the way.

○ Playa de la Concha rarely has surf, but even so, obey the summer lifeguards, because conditions change fast. For waves, head to nearby Playa de la Zurriola (p143) in Gros.

○ Parking close to the beach is very difficult (if not impossible) at peak times.

✕ Take a Break

There are lots of places to grab a snack or an ice cream around the beach; for the latter, try Arnoldo Heladeria (p134).

Built into the pavilions that back the beach is the art-deco Café de la Concha (p134), which has all-day dining and out-of-this-world views.

Top Experience
Enjoy Mountaintop Views at Monte Igueldo

MAP P130, A3

www.monteigueldo.es

At the far western end of the Bahía de la Concha is the fun-filled Monte Igueldo. Attractions include a funicular railway to the summit and a funfair. While this might sound like child's play, the views from the top are like nectar to lovers of sunsets. Clifftop coastal walks also provide inspiration for hikers to make the trip.

Funicular Railway

The **funicular railway** (Map p130, A3; www.monteigueldo.es) has been clattering up the side of Monte Igueldo since 1912, allowing you to enjoy old-world transport. It's the best option for accessing the glorious views from the top of the hill. It departs every 15 minutes.

The Views

The views from the summit of Monte Igueldo will make you feel like a circling hawk staring over the vast panorama of the Bahía de la Concha and the surrounding coastline and mountains.

Parque de Atracciones

At the **funfair** (www.monteigueldo.es) atop Monte Igueldo, individual attractions include roller coasters, boat rides and carousels. Each ride costs between €1 and €5. Opening hours fluctuate and the park usually only opens at weekends outside of summer; check the website for schedules.

Sunset

When the weather gods are smiling, Monte Igueldo is a fine place to be at sunset: watch as the orange sun drops into the ocean and the lighthouse adds its own light show.

Torreón de Monte Igueldo

The striking **Tower of Monte Igueldo** (www.monteigueldo.es/the-tower) is a fortified 16th-century lighthouse. It no longer works (there's a new lighthouse nearby), but it offers a great vantage point.

★ Top Tips

- The sweeping views from 181m-high Monte Igueldo over the Bahía de La Concha and Parte Vieja are worth the trip alone.

- Weekends, when local families come with children, might be the busiest times to visit, but are also the most festive.

- While there is a car park at the top, spaces are limited; it's easier to take the funicular.

✕ Take a Break

There are various cheap and cheerful **snack bars** at the top of Monte Igueldo.

Directly below Monte Igueldo, only steps from the funicular entrance, Restaurante Tenis Ondarreta (p135) serves inventive Basque cuisine. Along with the adjacent **Wimbledon English Pub**, it's part of San Sebastián Royal Tennis Club.

Walking Tour

Old & New in San Sebastián

Small, compact and very pedestrian-friendly, San Sebastián lends itself to gentle ambles. In the space of a few hundred metres you can pass by crowded pintxo bars, pretty churches, a couple of outrageously beautiful urban beaches, tempting designer clothes shops and some elegant bridges. This circular walk takes you through the best of the city centre.

Walk Facts

Start/Finish Parque de Alderdi Eder

Length 3.5km; three hours

❶ Parque de Alderdi Eder

Overlooking the magnificent Playa de la Concha, **Parque de Alderdi Eder** (p133) is the city's social centre. The park's trees and well-tended flowerbeds frame broad plazas and a lovely old carousel. Street performers flock here on weekends.

❷ Ayuntamiento

Once a casino, the **Ayuntamiento** (p133) is one of the most impressive buildings in San Sebastián, even if what goes on inside the city's town hall is less glamorous today.

❸ Basílica de Santa María del Coro

The intimate and artistic **Basílica de Santa María del Coro** (p113) is the Parte Vieja's best-loved church.

❹ Plaza de la Constitución

San Sebastián's most photogenic plaza, the Parte Vieja's **Plaza de la Constitución** (p115) once hosted bullfights. Today it's ringed by *pintxo* bars spilling onto outdoor terraces.

❺ Plaza de Gipuzkoa

It might be called a plaza, but with its duck-filled pond, flowerbeds and many trees, the 19th-century **Plaza de Gipuzkoa** (p132) is as much a formal garden park as a city square.

❻ Hotel Maria Cristina

Peek inside the lobby of the early 20th-century **Hotel Maria Cristina** (p132), whose first guest was the namesake regent of Spain. Today, the hotel is still one of the city's grandest, and is a riverside landmark.

❼ Kursaal

Cross the river via the **Puente de Zurriola** bridge to Gros and admire the **Kursaal** (p146) building, the city's modernist wonder. Opened in 1999, its design is said to represent two beached rocks. Head around the back to check out the surf on Playa de la Zurriola.

❽ Puente de Maria Cristina

Follow the river upstream along the Gros side to the prettiest bridge in the city, the **Puente de Maria Cristina** (p133). It's a belle époque creation most notable for its golden statues of winged angels atop rearing horses.

❾ Catedral del Buen Pastor de San Sebastián

From the Puente de Maria Cristina, on the new town side of the river, make your way to the city's magnificent **Catedral del Buen Pastor de San Sebastián** (p133), which was consecrated in 1897. Its stained-glass windows depict the 12 apostles.

San Sebastián New Town & Monte Igueldo

Mar Cantábrico (Kantauri Itsasoa)

Parque Igueldo
Punta Torrepea
• *Peine del Viento*
Paseo del Faro

Monte Igueldo
Funicular Railway
18
Plaza del Funicular
Av de Satrustegui
Paseo de Eduardo Chillida

Isla de Santa Clara

Bahía de la Concha (Kontxako Badia)

Playa de Ondarreta 2

Pico del Loro

Paseo de Igueldo
Av de Satrustegui
ONDARRETA
C de Brunet
C de Pamplona
Av de Zumalkarregi
C de Vitoria-Gasteiz
C de Matia
C de Erregezain

Plaza de Alfonso XIII
Jardines de Miramar
9
Palacio Miramar 3

Paseo de la Concha
Paseo de Miraconcha

27
ANTIGUO
29

For reviews see

◉	Top Experiences	p124
◉	Sights	p132
✖	Eating	p133
🅳	Drinking	p135
★	Entertainment	p138
🅷	Shopping	p138

0 — 500 m
0 — 0.25 miles

131

San Sebastián New Town & Monte Igueldo

GROS

PARTE VIEJA

- Fishing Port
- Paseo del Muelle
- C Marijuentea
- C Mayor
- C de San Juan
- C de Aldamar
- C de Salamanca
- Puente de Zurriola
- Paseo de Ramón María Lili
- Alameda del Boulevard
- Blvd Reina Regente
- Paseo de la República Argentina
- C de Okendo
- 28
- 34
- 12
- 5
- 26
- 4 ⊙ Hotel Maria Cristina
- Ayuntamiento 22
- 10
- 30
- C Sta Catalina
- Puente de Santa Catalina
- Parque de Alderdi Eder 6
- 31
- C Peñaflorida
- C de Hernani
- C Bengoechea
- Plaza de Gipuzkoa
- 17
- 32
- C de Garibai
- C Andia
- 11
- 33
- C de Etxaide
- C de Bergara
- Paseo de los Fueros
- Plaza de Cervantes
- Av de la Libertad
- C de Loyola
- C Hondarribia
- C Getaria
- Río Urumea
- 16
- 35
- C de San Martín
- Train Station (Renfe)
- Paseo de la Concha
- C de Urbieta
- C de Arasate
- C Valentín Olano
- 8 ⊙ Puente de Maria Cristina
- 14
- C de Zubieta
- C de Manterola
- Catedral del Buen Pastor de San Sebastián 7
- Plaza del Buen Pastor
- 25
- C del Triunfo
- 15
- C de la Marina
- C San Bartolomé
- 13
- 36
- 1
- 21
- 23
- Koldo Mitxelena Kulturunea
- C de Urdaneta
- Playa de la Concha
- 20
- La Perla Thalasso Sports Centre
- 19
- **CENTRO ROMÁNTICO**
- C de Larramendi
- C de Prim
- Reyes Católicos
- C de los Católicos
- C de Moraza
- Cuesta de Aldapeta
- Paseo de Árbol de Guernica
- C de Easo
- C de Egaña
- Parque Basoerdi
- Amara Train Station (ET/FV)

Sights

Koldo Mitxelena Kulturunea
CULTURAL CENTRE

1 MAP P130, G4

Set in a grand neoclassical building dating from the 1890s, this cultural centre has a packed line-up of art exhibitions, book launches, discussions and more. Don't miss the galleries downstairs, which mount free, thought-provoking exhibitions. The centre is named after Koldo Mitxelena, a writer and linguist, and one of the great champions of creating a unified Basque language. (http://kmk.gipuzkoakultura.eus)

Playa de Ondarreta
BEACH

2 MAP P130, B4

Playa de Ondarreta, the western extension of the renowned Playa de la Concha, has a less glam, more genteel atmosphere. It's long been popular with the city's most wealthy visitors and residents – look for the former royal summer palace of Miramar (p133) that overlooks the beach. Blue-and-white-striped canvas beach cabanas and volleyball nets dot the sands.

Jardines de Miramar
PARK

3 MAP P130, B4

Overlooking Playa de la Concha and Playa de Ondarreta, the grassy lawns of the Jardines de Miramar slope gently down to the ocean and are a popular place to catch some sun or have a picnic with a view beside the magnificent Palacio Miramar (p133).

Hotel Maria Cristina
HISTORIC BUILDING

4 MAP P130, H2

A wonderful example of belle époque architecture, the Hotel Maria Cristina was designed by Charles Mewes, the architect responsible for the Ritz hotels in Paris and London. It first opened its doors in 1912; the first guest was the regent of Spain, Maria Cristina. Today, anyone can enter the lobby and admire the understated luxury, or browse the items on sale at the Lukas Gourmet Shop (p138). (www.hotel-maria cristina.com)

Plaza de Gipuzkoa
PARK

5 MAP P130, G2

Designed in 1877 by French landscape artist Pierre Ducasse, who also created the Jardines de Miramar, this little park is one of San Sebastián's loveliest oases, with a duck pond, a little stream crossed by a small footbridge, and a waterfall. A small temple-like structure shelters a meteorological barometer and planetary chart; also here are two large clocks (one made of flowers) and a statue of pianist and composer José María Usandizaga.

Parque de Alderdi Eder PARK

6 MAP P130, F2

One of the most attractive and enjoyable little outdoor spaces in San Sebastián, the Parque de Alderdi Eder is actually more of an elongated plaza shaded by trees, dotted with benches and busy with children and families enjoying the old-fashioned carousel and, on weekends, street performers. Brilliant views unfold over Playa de la Concha.

Catedral del Buen Pastor de San Sebastián CATHEDRAL

7 MAP P130, G3

The dominant building of the new town is the city cathedral, overlooking a busy plaza. Built from slate and sandstone quarried from Monte Igueldo, the cathedral was consecrated in 1897 and has a 75m-high bell tower. Under the foundation stone of the cathedral is a lead box containing pictures of the Spanish royal family and the pope at the time of construction.

Puente de Maria Cristina BRIDGE

8 MAP P130, H3

Several bridges span the narrow Río Urumea, but by far the most impressive is the Puente de Maria Cristina. Opened in 1905, the belle époque structure is most notable for its four golden-statue-crowned obelisks, two of which guard the entrance on each side.

Palacio Miramar PALACE

9 MAP P130, C4

When a royal family comes to the seaside, they need a suitable summer beach pad. For Maria Cristina and family, that was the Palacio Miramar. It was built in the late 19th century in a 'Queen Anne English cottage' style (some cottage!), but sadly the interior is closed to the public.

Ayuntamiento HISTORIC BUILDING

10 MAP P130, F2

San Sebastián's town hall is an impressive configuration of belle époque towers and domed ceilings that stands proudly at the meeting point between Playa de la Concha, the Centro Romántico and the Parte Vieja. It began life as the Gran Casino in 1887, before becoming the town hall in 1947.

Eating

Antonio Bar BASQUE €€€

11 MAP P130, G2

From the outside, Antonio Bar looks like the sort of cafe you'd get in a train station waiting room. Hidden downstairs, however, is its six-table basement dining room (reserve ahead), where house speciality stews include *marmitako de bonito* (bonito, potato, red pepper and tomato) and *callos y morros* (beef tripe, blood sausage and chickpeas). *Pintxos* are served at the bar. (www.antoniobar.com)

Arnoldo Heladeria — ICE CREAM €

12 MAP P130, F2

In business since 1935, Arnoldo Heladeria makes San Sebastián's best ice cream. Alongside sorbets such as mango and passionfruit, and white peach, they make richer, creamier varieties like sherry-soaked raisin, salted walnut and chocolate-raspberry, plus ice lollies, milkshakes and frappés. From July to September, you can place orders over €12.50 by phone and collect them at beach pick-up points. (www.arnoldoheladeria.com)

Altuna — PINTXOS €€

13 MAP P130, F4

Decorated in jade-green tiles, this contemporary stunner serves freshly shucked oysters and inventive *pintxos,* such as dried tuna and cold almond soup served in a shot glass, and smoked prickly pear with *jamón* and orange dust. (https://altuna-boutique-bar.negocio.site)

Amelia — GASTRONOMY €€€

14 MAP P130, F3

While most of the Basque Country's Michelin-starred restaurants are located in small mountain villages, Amelia is located right beside the Playa de la Concha. Boasting two of the coveted stars, this tiny restaurant is officially a gourmand's paradise, blending traditional Basque with Italian and Japanese influences. The dining experience involves a set 14-course menu consisting mostly of seafood dishes. Dietary requirements cannot be accommodated. Book in advance. (www.ameliarestaurant.com)

Café de la Concha — BASQUE €€

15 MAP P130, E4

The Café de la Concha is inside a wonderful art-deco building that recalls San Sebastián's aristocratic heyday. As regal as the history are the views – you're almost sitting among the sunbathers on the beach. Alongside beach-cafe fare (breakfasts, salads, burgers) are more gourmet mains such as truffle potato gratin, tuna tataki with tomato jam or beef tenderloin with shiitake mushrooms and port sauce. (www.cafedelaconcha.com; 📶)

Rojo y Negro — PINTXOS €

16 MAP P130, F3

You can eat a full sit-down meal at this bar, but you're best following

---

> **Historic Spa**
>
> Halfway along the beachfront is the unmistakable white confection of **La Perla Thalasso Sports Centre** (Map p130, E4; www.la-perla.net), a highly rated spa that offers a comprehensive set of treatments inside a grand 1912 building dating from the belle époque ('beautiful era' in French, between the end of the Franco-Prussian War in 1871 and the outbreak of WWI in 1914).

the locals' lead and concentrating on *pintxos* such as prawn tacos with curry, homemade meatballs, grilled foie gras with banana compote and an ever-changing weekly special, washed down with a local *txakoli* or cider. For breakfast try the *tosta a la catalana:* toast, tomato, olive oil and garlic. (www.rojoynegrodonosti.es)

Kata.4   SEAFOOD €€€

17 MAP P130, H2

An urbane crowd gather at this fashionable spot near the ritzy Hotel Maria Cristina to feast on eight different varieties of oysters and refined *pintxos*, such as tempura softshell crab or pork cheeks. Seafood standouts on its restaurant menu include scallops with a Jerusalem artichoke puree and rock mussels in white wine. (www.kata4.com; 🛜)

Restaurante Tenis Ondarreta   BASQUE €€

18 MAP P130, A3

At the foot of Monte Igueldo, in the San Sebastián Royal Tennis Club, this restaurant has a white-dressed dining room and al fresco terrace overlooking the courts. Contemporary Basque dishes include garlicky salt-cod *pil-pil* with green-pepper sauce, grilled squid with caramelised onion and veal cutlets in an Idiazabal cheese sauce.

Start or end with a pint at the adjacent Wimbledon English Pub. (www.tenisondarreta.com)

Palacio Miramar (p133)

Casa Valles   PINTXOS €

19 MAP P130, G4

Well away from the tourist hustle and bustle is this timber-panelled locals' institution with long communal tables serving some of the new town's best *pintxos* beneath a forest of hung hams. Don't miss its *gildas* (a ubiquitous *pintxo* in northern Spain of anchovies, olives and pickled green peppers), allegedly invented here in 1948. (www.barvalles.com)

Drinking

Bataplan Disco   CLUB

20 MAP P130, E4

San Sebastián's top club, a classic disco housed in a grand seafront complex, sets the stage for memo-

Peine del Viento

A symbol of the city, the **Peine del Viento sculpture** (Wind Comb; Map p130, A2), which sits below Monte Igueldo at the far western end of the Bahía de la Concha, is the work of well-known Basque sculptor Eduardo Chillida and architect Luis Peña Ganchegui, and was installed in 1977. It makes for a great hour-long walk from the new town. On stormy days, waves crash between the rocks and add to the drama.

Gu
COCKTAIL BAR

22 MAP P130, F2

Glorious beach views extend from this waterfront cocktail bar in the 1929-opened Real Club Náutico de San Sebastián building, designed to look like a boat. It's a stunning setting for a sundowner on the terrace and late-night cocktails. The DJ-fuelled club gets going at midnight. (www.gusansebastian.com)

Pokhara
BAR

23 MAP P130, H4

A hip favourite near the cathedral, Pokhara draws a wide cross section of imbibers and party people to its weekend DJ sessions. During the week, it's a fine spot to relax with a well-made cocktail, especially at the al fresco tables in front. Try the house-speciality *carajillo*, a hot espresso served with cream and flaming whisky.

rable beachside partying. The club action kicks in late, but in summer you can warm up with a drink or two on the street-level terrace. Note that door selection can be arbitrary and groups of men might have trouble getting in. (www.facebook.com/bataplandiscooficial)

Old Town Coffee
COFFEE

21 MAP P130, G4

The name is a misnomer but this new-town place is spot-on for coffee. Set up by two Brazilian friends, it does small-batch roasting on site, and uses boutique roasts such as Nomad (Barcelona) and Square Mile (London) in a variety of brewing techniques, including pour-overs, Aeropress and V20. Fresh-squeezed juices and all-day breakfasts (eg avocado toast) are also available. (www.oldtowncoffeeroasters.com)

Museo del Whisky
BAR

24 MAP P130, G1

Appropriately named, this atmospheric bar is full of bottles of Scotland's finest (3400 bottles to be exact, though only 200 varieties are served) as well as a museum's worth of whisky-related knick-knacks – old bottles, mugs and glasses – displayed in timber-framed glass cabinets. Things really liven up once the pianist gets going. (www.facebook.com/museodelwhisky)

Botanika
CAFE

25 MAP P130, H3

Escape the beachfront hordes at this gem of a cafe. Housed in a river-facing residential block, it's popular with locals of all ages, who flock to the small, leafy patio and sunny, art-filled interior to chat over wine and vermouth. It also stages occasional live jazz, and DJs spin on Sundays. (www.facebook.com/KafeBotanika;)

Koh Tao
CAFE

26 MAP P130, G2

Good at any time of the day, Koh Tao is a laid-back place with mismatched vintage furniture, comfy armchairs, street-art murals on

---

Taste The Local Cider

For the Basques, cider came before wine. The cool, rain-soaked hills of the Basque Country are ideal for growing apples, and where you find apples, you can bet you'll find cider as well. Basque cider is generally considered 'natural', in that it's not sparkling like most other European ciders. In order to add a little fizz, the cider is poured from wooden barrels into the glass from about arm's height.

A *sagardotegi* (*sidrería* in Spanish) is a cider house, one of the great institutions of Basque life. A *sagardotegi* isn't just about drinking cider, however, as they also serve food. Traditionally, a meal starts with a cod omelette, before moving onto charcoal-grilled steaks the size of a cow and finishing with dessert, which is invariably the local Idiazabal cheese with walnuts.

A night in a *sagardotegi* can be great fun for a group. The average cost of a meal is around €25 to €30 per person, which includes all the cider you can drink. Tradition states that each group of diners has someone who calls out '*txotx*' at regular intervals. This is your cue to get up from the table and head to the big barrels for a refill, where either a barman or the leader of your group opens the tap and everyone takes turns filling up before heading back to the table.

Cider season is January to April, but it's possible to visit a number of cider orchards, manufacturers and cider houses year-round. Find locations online at www.sagardoa.eus or ask at the **Sagardoetxea** (www.sagardoarenlurraldea.eus), a cider museum where you can tour an orchard, taste a tipple of cider and learn all you ever wanted to know about the drink. It's located on the edge of the little town of Astigarraga, 6km south of San Sebastián, which happens to be one of the Basque Country's best places to find a *sagardotegi*. Buses A1 and A2 run here from San Sebastián-Donostia Amara station (€1.85, 25 minutes, every 15 minutes).

Riverside Walks

The Río Urumea runs through the middle of San Sebastián, separating the new town from the Gros neighbourhood. The river is largely overlooked by visitors, but locals love to stroll the walkways that run along the banks, scattered with small areas of parkland and children's playgrounds.

its exposed-brick walls and good tunes. It's the ideal spot to unwind over a coffee or kick back with an early evening beer, wine or cocktail.

La Mera Mera · BAR

27 · MAP P130, A5

Just off the beaten path, La Mera Mera is a shoebox-sized bar with a bohemian air thanks to the old photos on the walls and slender brassy light fixtures. The cocktails are excellent (especially the strong margaritas), while you can sip a range of fine tequilas and mezcals. A menu of Mexican snacks includes a smash-your-own guacamole (you're given a mortar and pestle). (www.lameramera.es)

Entertainment

Teatro Victoria Eugenia · THEATRE

28 · MAP P130, G1

Built in 1912 and refurbished between 2001 and 2007, the city's belle époque theatre presents a varied collection of theatre and classical music. A frescoed dome crowns its main hall, which has a capacity of 910 people. (www.victoriaeugenia.eus)

Doka · LIVE MUSIC

29 · MAP P130, B5

Catch live music in a wide range of genres – everything from Basque folk to rock, metal and pop – as well as theatre performances, poetry readings and comedy. The small venue is in a residential backstreet just south of Playa de Ondarreta. (www.doka.eus)

Shopping

Perfumería Benegas · PERFUME

30 · MAP P130, G2

Founded in 1908, Benegas stocks leading international brands and in-house creations such as Ssirimiri, which uses San Sebastián as its inspiration – the rains, sunshine and sea breezes all packaged in one lovely box (featuring iconic imagery of the city). You'll also find make-up and gents' grooming products. (www.perfumeriabenegas.com)

Lukas Gourmet Shop · FOOD & DRINKS

Located inside the regal Hotel Maria Cristina, this is where those with a real appreciation of fine food and wine come to do their shopping. The shop (see **4** Map p130, H2) also offers customised hampers and international shipping, as well as a wide selection of edible souvenirs, tableware and gourmet gifts. Check out sister company Mimo's foodie **tours** (https://mimo.eus) and cooking classes as well. (https://lukasgourmet.com)

Loreak Mendian   CLOTHING

31 MAP P130, G2

Basque label Loreak Mendian specialises in affordable style for men and women – everything from T-shirts and hoodies to dresses and lightweight sweaters. This branch carries both menswear and women's fashions in a crisp, minimalist setting. (www.loreakmendian.com)

Erviti   MUSICAL INSTRUMENTS

32 MAP P130, H2

Erviti has published Basque musical scores since it was established in 1875. Now run by the fifth generation, it stocks traditional Basque musical instruments, including an *alboka* (single-reed woodwind instrument), *txistu* (three-holed wooden pipe), *ttun-ttun* (six-stringed instrument named for the sound it makes) and a *kirikoketa* and *txalaparta* (both wooden percussion instruments similar to xylophones). (https://erviti.negocio.site)

Chocolates de Mendaro   CHOCOLATE

33 MAP P130, H2

It's all but impossible to walk past this fabulous old chocolate shop and resist the temptation to step inside. The famed chocolatier has been around since 1850 and is still run by the Saint-Gerons family. (www.chocolatesdemendaro.com)

Elkano 1 Gaztagune   CHEESE

34 MAP P130, G2

Over 40 different artisan cheeses fill this aromatic little timber-lined shop. Most are from the Basque Country, including the owner's own Idiazabal (pressed sheep's milk cheese); there are also a handful of varieties from France, Italy, the Netherlands and Scotland. (www.facebook.com/elkano1gaztagune)

Mercado San Martín   MARKET

35 MAP P130, G3

Originally built in 1884, Mercado San Martín was replaced with a gleaming modern structure in 2005. At street level you'll find butchers, greengrocers, florists and an excellent bakery (its hot, savoury pastries make great on-the-go snacks), as well as cafes. Downstairs is a large fishmonger's hall filled with locally caught seafood. (www.mercadosanmartin.es)

Goiuri   FASHION & ACCESSORIES

36 MAP P130, G4

If you're looking for a new statement-making swimsuit to wear on the beach, head to Goiuri. It stocks its own bikinis and one-pieces for women and Sargori board shorts for men, which it designs and produces locally, as well as women's swimwear from Australian brand Seafolly. (www.goiuri.com)

Explore
San Sebastián Gros

The seaside neighbourhood of Gros is cool, young and pure surf fashion. The neighbourhood largely lacks the architectural pleasures of other parts of town, but with a spectacular beach, some of the best-value hotels in the city and a reputation as a pintxo powerhouse (especially at the pintxo-pote on Thursday evenings), you're likely to spend a lot of time having fun here.

The Short List

- **Playa de la Zurriola (p143)** Strolling Gros' sweeping surf beach at sunset.
- **Parque de Cristina Enea (p143)** Escaping the crowds in the city's prettiest park, among peacocks, towering trees and expanses of lawn.
- **Kursaal (p146)** Checking out the futuristic design – two cubes made of translucent glass with LED lights – of architect Rafael Moneo's striking cultural centre.
- **Bodega Donostiarra (p144)** Dining on bite-size delights at stops like this along the restaurant-lined streets of Zabaleta and Peña y Goñi.
- **Pukas Surf Eskola (p143)** Hiring a board, or taking a class, to ride the waves lapping at Gros' doorstep.

Getting There & Around

✈ Gros is just over the Puente de Zurriola (Zurriola Bridge), which leads to the Parte Vieja and the new town. There's no need to use public transport to get here.

San Sebastián Gros Map on p142

Playa de la Zurriola (153) BORIS STROUJKO/SHUTTERSTOCK ©

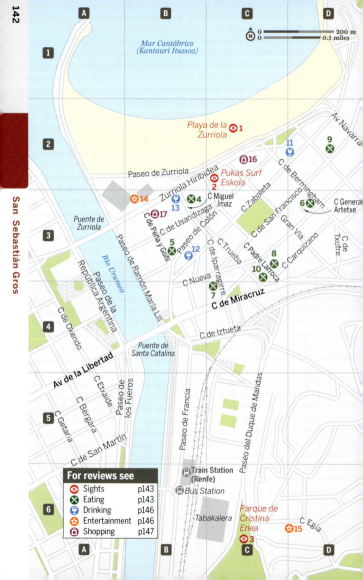

Sights

Playa de la Zurriola BEACH

1 MAP P142, C2

Stretching 800m in front of Gros, from the Kursaal to Monte Ulía, 'Zurri', as it's known locally, has some excellent waves that draw surfers from near and far. It's a superb place to hang out and take in the local scene of volleyball, football and surf action; swimming here is at its best when there's no swell.

Pukas Surf Eskola SURFING

2 MAP P142, C2

Aspiring surfers should drop by Pukas. Prices for classes vary depending on duration and group size, but start at €71 for a weekend course comprising a 1½-hour lesson each day. Boards and wetsuits are available for hire. (https://eskola.pukassurf.com)

Parque de Cristina Enea PARK

3 MAP P142, C6

Created by the Duke of Mandas in honour of his wife, the Parque de Cristina Enea is a favourite escape for locals.

This formal park, the most attractive in the city, contains ornamental plants, ducks and peacocks, and open lawns.

Its wooded paths make for a scenic stroll, past towering red sequoias and a magnificent Lebanese cedar.

San Sebastián to Pasaia on Foot

A rewarding way of reaching **Pasaia** (p149) is to walk the coastal path from San Sebastián. This 7.7km trail, part of the Camino del Norte (p152), takes about three hours and passes patches of forest and unusual cliff formations, offering lovely sea views. Halfway along, a hidden beach, **Playa de Murgita**, tempts when it's hot.

From San Sebastián, the route starts at the eastern end of Gros' Playa de la Zurriola, at the top of the steps leading from Calle de Zemoria up Monte Ulía. From Pasaia it climbs past the lighthouse on the northwestern side of the port.

Eating

Xarma BASQUE €€€

4 MAP P142, B3

A striking contemporary wood-lined dining room with bare-bulb downlights is the backdrop for artistically presented dishes prepared in the open kitchen.

A meal might start with watermelon gazpacho with melon-filled cucumber cannelloni, followed by smoked Basque trout with Ossau-Iraty sheep's cheese, fresh herbs and honey, or suckling pig's trotters with roast onion cream and caramelised figs. (www.xarmacook.com)

Bodega Donostiarra
PINTXOS €

5 MAP P142, B3

The whitewashed stone walls, framed prints and black-and-white photos give this place a quirky charm, though the crowds can be so thick that you might not even notice during prime time.

The draw? Some of the best *pintxos* this side of the Urumea: seared mackerel with salmon roe, black pudding with sweet red peppers, or grilled chorizo and octopus skewers. (www.bodegadonostiarra.com)

Bergara Bar
PINTXOS €

6 MAP P142, D3

The Bergara Bar is one of Gros' most highly regarded *pintxo* bars and has a mouth-watering array of delights piled on the bar counter, as well as others chalked on the board.

You can't go wrong, whether you opt for its anchovy tortilla, *chupito* (spider-crab mousse served in a shot glass) or the Donostiarra, an elaborate alternative to the *gilda* (pintxo of olive, anchovy and pickled pepper), with cod. (www.pinchosbergara.es)

Gerald's Bar
INTERNATIONAL €€

7 MAP P142, C4

Melbourne-based restaurateur Gerald Diffey fell so hard for San

Pintxos in Bergara Bar

Sebastián that he decided to open a second Gerald's in the city – never mind that the first is 17,000km away.

The menu changes daily but might feature steak-and-kidney pie, smoked duck breast with fig and red-onion chutney, or roast butternut squash with labneh (yogurt) and pistachio pesto. (www.geraldsbar.eu)

La Txuleteria BASQUE €€€

8 MAP P142, C3

For meat lovers, La Txuleteria is the Basque Country's ultimate steakhouse. Hot iron plates heaped with sizzling T-bones are served direct to the table, but the side dishes aren't overlooked.

You'll find one of the city's best tomato salads and Padrón pepper plates here.

Wild mushrooms picked in the surrounding hills are a welcome addition during the autumn months. Find it on Facebook.

Alabama Café HEALTH FOOD €

9 MAP P142, D2

At this cosy cafe, everything is prepared fresh to order, including acai bowls overflowing with fruit and dozens of healthy juices and smoothies.

The breakfast menu options prove excellent value and the coffee is always top quality.

The cafe's limited space is used well, with additional seating outside and upstairs on a mezzanine floor overlooked by colourful murals.

Plenty of vegan and gluten-free options are available. (https://byalabama.com;)

Pintxo-Pote in Gros

Every Thursday, the streets of Gros come alive with revellers making a habitual bar crawl sampling *pintxos* and drinks at a discounted price between 7pm and 10pm. Known as the *pintxo-pote*, you'll find that most bars in the neighbourhood take part. Usually only certain *pintxos* are included. Ask bar staff for guidance. Prices range between €3 and €5 for a drink and a *pintxo*. Crowds are biggest to the eastern end of Calle Zabaleta.

Mapa Verde VEGAN €€

10 MAP P142, C3

This popular vegan spot epitomises the progressive vibe of the Gros neighbourhood.

Sustainable and healthy dishes range from hearty Buddha bowls to elegantly presented concoctions such as tempeh salad with cashew cheese, basil and mango.

Save room for the excellent tiramisu. (www.mapaverdedonostia.com;)

Drinking

Mala Gissona Beer House
CRAFT BEER

11 MAP P142, D2

The long wooden bar, industrial fixtures and inviting front terrace make a suitable backdrop to the dozen quality brews on tap here.

Half are from its own brewery in nearby Oiartzun, such as Nao (pale ale) and Django (blanche), while the rest are from other Basque and international brewers.

Soak them up with bar food including fantastic burgers. (www.malagissona.beer; 📶)

Cultural Hub Tabakalera

Sun-drenched cultural space **Tabakalera** (Map p142, C6; www.tabakalera.eu) occupies a beautifully reconfigured tobacco factory. It's a hub for the arts and design, as well as cultural enterprises such as the Basque Film Archive, the Kutxa Foundation and various galleries and innovative firms. For visitors, there's also an exhibition hall, a cinema and a regular line-up of seminars, workshops, discussions and other edifying fare. There are great views from the rooftop glass-prism terrace. Find listings on their website.

La Gintonería Donostiarra
BAR

12 MAP P142, B3

A much-loved drinking spot in Gros, this gin joint has more than 100 varieties of the good stuff, and makes one of the best (and biggest!) gin and tonics in town.

The all-white interior is light, bright and contemporary; on warm days, the best seats are out on the terrace. (www.facebook.com/LaGintoneriaDonostiarra; 📶)

Ondarra
BAR

13 MAP P142, B3

Across the road from Playa de la Zurriola, Ondarra draws a chilled-out surf crowd. Live music gigs often take place in the basement. (www.ondarra.eus)

Entertainment

Kursaal
LIVE PERFORMANCE

14 MAP P142, B3

An energetic and exciting array of performances are staged inside the **Kursaal** (www.kursaal.eus) centre, an architectural landmark dating to 1999.

Everything from symphonic concerts and musicals to dance performances and rock shows features; check out the website for upcoming events. (www.kursaal.eus)

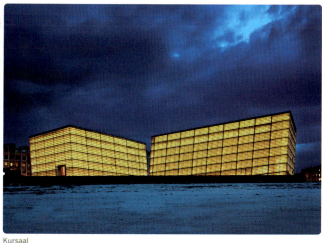

Kursaal

Le Bukowski
LIVE MUSIC

15 ⭐ MAP P142, D6

Live bands take the stage most nights at this nightspot, which also has DJs spinning a wide range of sounds – funk, hip-hop, soul, rock.

It's located south of Gros near the mainline train station. (www.lebukowski.com; 📶)

Shopping

Lauter
ALCOHOL

16 🔒 MAP P142, C2

You can buy Basque and guest international craft beers to take away at Lauter, or fill a takeaway bottle (500ml or 1000ml) from one of its 18 taps and head to the beach (it's not licensed for drinking on site). (www.instagram.com/lauterbeers)

soule.
FASHION & ACCESSORIES

17 🔒 MAP P142, B3

On one of Gros' liveliest lanes, this women's wear boutique is a great place to hit up when you need a new piece for your travel wardrobe. Browse for soft linen shirts, oversized patterned sweaters, floral dresses and rugged canvas bags with leather straps. (https://soule.es)

Explore
Hondarribia & Pasaia

With its walled Casco Histórico (Historic Centre), buzzing beach scene and fabulous eateries, Hondarribia makes for a wonderful day trip, or longer visit. The town, 20km from San Sebastián on the French border, lies to the east of the historic port of Pasaia.

The Short List

○ **Casco Histórico (p151)** Wandering through Hondarribia's historic core.

○ **Ermita de Guadalupe (p152)** Hiking up to this hilltop hermitage to take in magnificent views.

○ **Hendaye (p155)** Hopping aboard the ferry from Hondarribia to this beautiful sandy beach across the border in France.

○ **Albaola Foundation (p153)** Learning about Pasaia's whaling history at this fascinating maritime museum.

○ **Camino del Norte (p152)** Following the conch shells to experience a slice of long-distance hiking culture.

Getting There & Around

🚌 Buses link Hondarribia's Calle Sabin Arana Goiri with the bus station in San Sebastián (E20 and E21, €2.65, 25 minutes, every 25 minutes).

⛴ To cross over to France, take the Hendaye–Hondarribia passenger ferry. The ferry is usually cancelled during strong winds.

Hondarribia & Pasaia Map on p150

Hondarribia ROMAN BELOGORODOV/SHUTTERSTOCK ©

Sights

Casco Histórico OLD TOWN

1 MAP P150, A5

Hondarribia's walled historic centre, much of which dates to the 15th and 16th centuries, is an atmospheric grid of graceful plazas, cobbled lanes, and buildings adorned with wood-carved eaves and wrought-iron balconies.

The focal square is **Plaza de Armas**, where you'll find the local **tourist office** (Map p150, B5; www.hondarribiaturismo.com), but prettier still is picture-perfect **Plaza de Gipuzkoa**.

Playa de Hondarribia BEACH

2 MAP P150, C1

Hondarribia's sheltered beach is lined with bars and restaurants, and offers calm swimming waters. When the swell is running, there's a long right-hand surf break off the breakwater.

Located 2km north of the new town (La Marina), the beach is popular with locals, but foreign tourists are rare.

Calle San Pedro STREET

3 MAP P150, C4

The main drag of Hondarribia's La Marina district, Calle San Pedro is a quaint pedestrian-only strip flanked by traditional fishers' houses, with facades painted bright green or blue, and wooden

Calle San Pedro

balconies cheerfully decorated with flower boxes.

Many of the old-fashioned buildings now contain *pintxo* bars and restaurants.

Ermita de Guadalupe — CHAPEL

4 MAP P150, A6

It's a hefty hike from Hondarribia – a 4km walk uphill – but the Ermita de Guadalupe is well worth the effort it takes to reach it (you can also drive) and has stunning views. Destroyed and rebuilt many times over the centuries, the hermitage's present structure dates from the 19th century.

Pick up a walking trail map from the tourist office. A pilgrimage takes place here on 8 September.

> ### Camino del Norte
>
> The first section of the Camino del Norte, a branch of the Camino de Santiago, runs from the French border at Irun to Pasaia. You can pick it up at the **Ermita de Guadalupe**, where you will see the conch-shell signs denoting the trail, and walk a section to Pasaia. There are two routes (each around 14km): a challenging one over the hilltops offering panoramic coastline views, and a gentler one through the forest. The route is well signposted.

Castillo de Carlos V — CASTLE

5 MAP P150, B5

Today it's a government-run hotel, but for over 1000 years this castle hosted knights and kings. Its position atop the old town hill gave it a commanding view over the strategic Bidasoa estuary, which has long marked the Spain–France border. Poke your head into the reception lobby to admire the medieval decor. (Plaza de Armas 14)

Eating

Gastroteka Danontzat — BASQUE €€

6 MAP P150, B5

Gastroteka Danontzat's fun, creative approach to dining combines beautifully prepared market-fresh fare with highly original presentation and props. Start off with smoked sardines, anchovies or crab croquettes, before moving on to tender tuna ceviche, squid cooked in its own ink or char-grilled entrecôte in red-pepper sauce. Small servings mean you can try a lot of flavours. (www.gastrotekadanontzat.com)

Laía Erretegia — GRILL €€€

7 MAP P150, A6

Chef Jon Ayala and his maître d' sister Arantza transformed these former stables into an open-plan dining space with glass cabinets where beef is aged for 30 to 60 days, wraparound shelves are

Pop Across to Pasaia

Where the river Oiartzun meets the Atlantic, Pasaia (Spanish: Pasajes) is both a massive industrial port and a sleepy village with quaint medieval houses hunkering over the waterfront.

In fact, it comprises four distinct districts, though it's Pasai San Pedro and Pasai Donibane that have all the charm for most visitors to the area.

These two villages face each other on opposite sides of the river, linked by a frequent, three-minute **ferry** (Map p150) ride, and are sprinkled with sights that pay homage to the region's maritime history.

The **Albaola Foundation** (www.albaola.com) charts the history of Pasaia's whaling industry. At the centre of the story is the *San Juan*, a galleon that sunk off the coast of Newfoundland in 1565.

Models and explanatory panels describe the ship and illustrate how a team of Canadian underwater archaeologists discovered its wreck in 1978.

The highlight, though, is the life-size replica of the ship being built using the same techniques and materials that were used to construct the original.

Over on the Pasai Donibane side, cobbled alleys wind past historic buildings to the **Plaza de Santiago**.

This cheerful pedestrian space is backed by a charmingly ramshackle cluster of narrow, tall buildings with colourful wooden balconies.

Cafe tables spill out into the square overlooking the busy waterfront.

Seafood is the star of the area's menus. Managed by the same family since 1884, **Casa Cámara** (www.casacamara.com) is built half on stilts over the harbour.

The majority of the menu is seafood based and the cooking is assured and traditional.

The lobsters live in a cage lowered down through a hole in the middle of the dining area straight into the water.

Buses link Hondarribia with Pasai San Pedro (€2.65, 30 minutes, every 30 minutes).

You can also reach Pasai San Pedro directly from San Sebastián's bus station (€1.85, 10 minutes, every 30 minutes) or on foot (p143) from Gros (7.6km).

stocked with wine, and floor-to-ceiling windows overlook the surrounding farmland and mountains. Steaks and daily caught seafood are grilled over charcoal; vegetables come from within a 30km radius. (www.laiaerretegia.com)

Gran Sol PINTXOS €€

8 MAP P150, C4

Wine barrels double as tables out the front of Gran Sol, one of Hondarribia's best-known addresses for *pintxos*. Standouts include mushrooms filled with cheese mousse, smoked cod with foie gras and peach jam, and pork with creamy mash and caramel.

Along with *txakoli* and other local wines, it has a range of Basque craft beers. (www.bargransol.com)

La Hermandad de Pescadores SEAFOOD €€€

9 MAP P150, C4

Housed in a traditional white-and-blue cottage, this institution dating to 1938 serves an array of seafood classics.

It's best known for its *sopa de pescado* (fish soup), said by some to be the best in the area. Book ahead where possible. (www.hermandaddepescadores.com)

Alameda BASQUE €€€

10 MAP P150, C6

Michelin-starred Alameda helped pave the way to Hondarribia becoming the culinary hotspot it is today.

What started life as a simple tavern is now a sophisticated

Pasaia (p153)

fine-dining restaurant, complete with a garden and terrace, serving creative takes on traditional Basque cuisine, prepared with fresh, locally sourced ingredients. (www.restaurantealameda.net)

Drinking

Vinoteka Ardoka
WINE BAR

11 MAP P150, C3

Behind its rustic stone facade, this contemporary wine bar has 30 wines by the glass, including locally produced *txakoli*, and reds and rosés from La Rioja, as well as over a dozen varieties of vermouth. Pair them with *pintxos* such as *txipiron* (squid-ink croquettes), *bacalao confitado* (confit cod) and *brocheta de langostinos* (shrimp skewers). (www.ardokavinoteka.com)

Amona Margarita
CAFE

12 MAP P150, C4

With a light, airy interior, this cafe-bakery is a lovely place to rejuvenate with a freshly squeezed juice, coffee or home-baked cake. (www.amonamargarita.com;)

Take a Ferry Trip to Hendaye

Just across the river from Hondarribia lies the pretty French town of **Hendaye** (Map p150, D3; France), linked by a regular passenger **ferry** (Map p150, C4; www.jolaski.com). Hendaye's main attraction is its 3km-long stretch of white-sand beach, a 250m stroll north of the ferry dock. It is a popular place for those learning to surf thanks to the gentler lineups and profusion of surf schools.

Shopping

Conservas Hondarribia
FOOD & DRINKS

13 MAP P150, B5

Everything at this light, bright deli is sourced from independent farms local to Hondarribia: salted anchovies, tinned sardines, clams and octopus, cheeses, preserved chillies, vinegar, oils, honey, chocolate, ciders, *txacoli* wines and more. (www.conservashondarribia.com)

Walking Tour

St-Jean-de-Luz, France

A short hop across the French border, St-Jean-de-Luz is a picturesque seaside village with a lively waterfront, impressive historic sights, and narrow cobblestone lanes that invite exploring. While this 1km walk takes around an hour, you could easily make a day of it, hanging out at the beach, followed by dining and drinking at the town's superb seafood restaurants.

Getting There

🚌 Flixbus (www.flixbus.fr) connects St-Jean-de-Luz with San Sebastián's bus station (€6–7 one way, 40 minutes, four daily).

🚗 Take the AP8, which becomes the A63 as you cross into France.

❶ Les Halles Centrales

Dating from 1884, the town's grand **market** offers a delight for the senses, with its vendors selling fresh fruits, cheeses, cured meats, breads and pastries. A corner food stall serves grilled sardines, oysters and refreshing wine.

❷ Église St-Jean Baptiste

The plain facade of France's largest Basque **church** (www.paroissespo.com/eglise-st-jean-baptiste-st-jean-de-luz) conceals a splendid interior with a magnificent baroque altarpiece. Louis XIV and María Teresa, daughter of King Philip IV of Spain, married here in 1660.

❸ Maison Adam

At the entrance to lively shopping and dining strip rue de la République, **Maison Adam** (www.maisonadam.fr) has been selling delicious *gâteau basque* (Basque cake filled with almond cream or preserved cherries) since 1666. It also has macarons, wines and preserves.

❹ Maison Louis XIV

The grandest house in town is the **Maison Louis XIV** (www.maison-louis-xiv.fr), where Louis XIV lived out his last days of bachelorhood. It was built in 1643 by a wealthy shipowner, and is awash with period detail and antiques. Guided tours leave several times daily from early April until early November.

❺ Fishing Port

Centuries of history lie hidden in this colourful **fishing port**. From here ships headed off to hunt whales off the frigid coast of Newfoundland in the 16th century. Although Saint-Jean-de-Luz has been a resort since the 19th century, it still has an active fishing fleet – though these days it goes after a smaller catch.

❻ Maison de l'Infante

In the days before her marriage to Louis XIV, María Teresa stayed in this brick-and-stone **mansion**, just off place Louis XIV. Like her husband-to-be's temporary home, it was constructed by a shipowner. It is closed to visitors.

❼ Grande Plage

The lovely crescent-shaped sands of the **Grande Plage** make a fine setting for a bit of downtime. Protected from the battering waves of the Atlantic by three breakwaters, the beach usually has calm waters, perfect for young swimmers. A long elevated promenade offers beautiful views over the seaside.

Survival Guide

Before You Go 160
Book Your Stay 160
When to Go 160

Arriving in Bilbao & San Sebastián 161
Bilbao Airport 161
San Sebastián Airport 161
Biarritz Airport 162
From the Train Stations 162
From the Bus Stations 162

Getting Around 162
Bilbao Metro 162
Bilbao Tram 163
Bus 163
Car 163
Taxi 163

Essential Information 163
Accessible Travel 163
Business Hours 164
Electricity 164
LGBTIQ+ Travellers 164
Money 165
Public Holidays 165
Safe Travel 166
Tourist Information 166
Visas 167

Bermeo Port (p95) IVAN SOTO COBOS/SHUTTERSTOCK ©

Before You Go

Book Your Stay

- Hotel rooms are at a premium in Basque Country, particularly in San Sebastián.
- Availability in high season is tight. During Easter and from June to September, book months in advance for the best options.

Useful Websites

- **Lonely Planet** (lonelyplanet.com/spain/hotels) Recommendations and bookings.
- **Tourism Euskadi** (www.tourism.euskadi.eus) The Basque tourist board gives lots of accommodation suggestions.
- **Bilbao Turismo** (www.bilbaoturismo.net) Accommodation bookings from Bilbao's tourism authority.
- **San Sebastián Turismo** (www.sansebastianturismo.com) Bookings from San Sebastián's tourism authority.

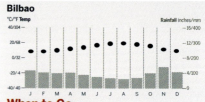

When to Go

- **Spring (Mar–May)** Unpredictable, sometimes very wet weather. May is more reliably sunny. Tourist crowds are low.
- **Summer (Jun–Sep)** Hot, endless festivals. Waves of tourists, higher prices.
- **Autumn (Oct & Nov)** October can be glorious, but by November winter is coming.
- **Winter (Dec–Feb)** Wet, often cold. Some sights are closed or operate on reduced hours.

- **Feel Free Rentals** (www.feelfreerentals.com) San Sebastián–based outfit renting apartments in and near the city.

Best Budget

Poshtel Bilbao (www.poshtelbilbao.com) Flashpacker base with first-rate facilities including a restaurant, bar and sauna.

Quartier Bilbao (www.quartierbilbao.com) A good-value penny pincher in Bilbao's old quarter.

Koba (www.kobahostel.com) Surfer-friendly hostel in San Sebastián's Gros neighbourhood.

Itsasmin Ostatua (www.itsasmin.com) In the hillside village of Elantxobe.

Pensión Txiki Polit (www.txikipolit.eus) Old-fashioned charm close to the beach in Zarautz's old town.

Best Midrange

Pensión Altair (www.pension-altair.com) Converted San Sebastián townhouse near the eateries of Gros.

Pensión Aldamar (www.pensionaldamar.

com) Professionally run, contemporary guesthouse in an excellent San Sebastián location.

Pensión Iturrienea Ostatua (www.iturrieneaostatua.com) Whimsically decorated *pensión* in Bilbao's old town; full of good cheer.

Casual Bilbao Gurea (www.casualhoteles.com) Family-run guesthouse near some great eating options in Bilbao's old town.

Hotel Ilunion Bilbao (www.ilunionbilbao.com) Well-priced contemporary hotel with all the essentials for a relaxing stay.

Hotel Zubieta (www.hotelzubieta.com) Lovely boutique hotel in the seaside village of Lekeitio.

Best Top End

Hotel Carlton (www.hotelcarlton.es) Grande dame of Bilbao with classic rooms and top-notch service.

Hotel Maria Cristina (www.hotel-mariacristina.com) The most famous address in San Sebastián, with stellar service and lavish rooms.

Miró Hotel (www.mirohotelbilbao.com) Stylish boutique accommodation across from the Museo Guggenheim Bilbao.

Gran Hotel Domine (www.granhoteldominebilbao.com) Luxury Bilbao hotel with all the frills, including a scenic roof terrace.

Hotel de Londres y de Inglaterra (www.hlondres.com) A majestic hotel with mesmerising views over San Sebastián's Playa de la Concha.

Hotel Iturregi (www.hoteliturregi.com) Ultracontemporary opulence in the hills above Getaria with sweeping Basque Coast views.

Arriving in Bilbao & San Sebastián

Bilbao Airport

o Bilbao Airport (www.aena.es) is 13km northeast of the centre.

o The **airport bus** departs from a stand on the extreme right as you leave arrivals.

o It travels through the northwestern section of the city, passing the Museo Guggenheim Bilbao, stopping at Plaza de Federico Moyúa and terminating at the Intermodal bus station.

o Services run from the airport every 15 minutes to 30 minutes from 6.15am to midnight.

o There is also a direct hourly bus from the airport to San Sebastián's bus station, adjacent to the mainline train station (€17.10, 1¼ hours). It runs every 30 minutes from 7.15am to 11.45pm.

o Taxis from the airport to the Casco Viejo cost about €30 to €35 depending on traffic.

San Sebastián Airport

o San Sebastián Airport (www.aena.es) is 22km east of town, near Hondarribia.

o It is a domestic airport serving Madrid and Barcelona.

o Buses E20 and E21 run hourly to San Sebastián's bus station (€2.65, 30 minutes), stopping at Plaza de Gipuzkoa.

- A taxi from the airport to the city centre costs about €35 to €45.

Biarritz Airport

- Biarritz Airport (www.biarritz.aeroport.fr), 48km northeast of San Sebastián in France, is a convenient arrival point for the region.
- Destinations served include the UK, Ireland and major continental European cities from spring to autumn.
- Buses (€7, 45 minutes, up to eight daily) link the airport with San Sebastián's bus station.

From the Train Stations

- Bilbao's Abando train station is just across the river from Plaza Arriaga and the Casco Viejo.
- Most accommodation is an easy walk away, but if you're staying near the Museo Guggenheim Bilbao, you might consider taking the tram or a taxi.
- San Sebastián's train station is a 10-minute walk south of the Parte Vieja; most people simply walk to their hotel or take a taxi.

From the Bus Stations

- Bilbao's main bus station, Intermodal, is west of the centre. You can easily walk to hotels in the new town, but for elsewhere consider a taxi or the metro (the nearest station is San Mamés, 100m or so away).
- San Sebastián's bus station is 1km southeast of the Parte Vieja, on the east side of the river, below the main train station.

Getting Around

Bilbao Metro

- Bilbao has a fast and efficient metro system that runs along two separate lines. There are stations at all the main focal points of El Ensanche and Casco Viejo.

Basque Country Place & Street Names

The vast majority of places in the Basque Country have Basque-language names rather than Spanish (Castilian) ones (for example, Gernika rather than Guernica). A few places, however, retain Spanish as the primary spelling, the most notable being Bilbao (Basque: Bilbo) and San Sebastián (Basque: Donostia).

Street names in larger cities, towns and villages in the Basque Country use both Spanish and Basque. The street name is preceded by the Spanish, and followed by the Basque, for example 'Calle Correo Kalea' (*calle* is Spanish for 'street', while *kalea* is Basque for 'street'). In small villages, street names are sometimes only in Basque.

- Tickets cost €1.70 to €1.95 (€0.48 to €0.62 with a Barik card), depending on the number of zones.

Bilbao Tram

- Bilbao's tram line runs between Basurtu, in the southwest of the city, and the Atxuri train station.

- Stops include the Intermodal bus station, the Museo Guggenheim Bilbao and Teatro Arriaga by the Casco Viejo.

- Tickets cost €1.50 (€0.73 with a Barik card) and need to be validated in the machine next to the ticket dispenser before boarding.

Bus

- Not many tourists use the city buses in either Bilbao or San Sebastián. However, bus 16 provides a painless way of getting from San Sebastián city centre to the base of Monte Igueldo via Playa de la Concha.

- Tickets cost €1.85 (€2.50 at night); you can pay the driver directly.

Car

- If you're simply staying put in Bilbao or San Sebastián then forget about hiring a car. It will cost a lot in parking fees and you won't need it in either city.

- If, however, you're planning on making a number of day trips, a car is a godsend as intercity buses and trains can be irregular.

- There are numerous underground car parks in both cities plus metered parking (expect to pay upwards of €25 for a full day).

- Parking in San Sebastián in summer can be virtually impossible, even at parking stations.

- City hotels generally charge for parking spots.

Taxi

- Taxis in Bilbao and San Sebastián are only available by reservation or at ranks; you can't hail them in the street.

- In Bilbao, try Teletaxi (944 10 21 21; www.teletaxibilbao.com).

- In San Sebastián, try Taxi Donosti (943 46 46 46; www.taxidonosti.com).

Barik Card

Save money by purchasing a Barik card for €3 at metro vending machines, topping it up with credit (from €5) and using it on Bilbao's metro, tram and bus lines. One card can be used for multiple people, and the card pays for itself after five uses. Single passes can also be purchased from metro machines.

- Expect to pay around €10 to cross central Bilbao or San Sebastián. Rates rise after dark.

Essential Information

Accessible Travel

Most sights in both Bilbao and San Sebastián are wheelchair accessible. However, many cheaper hotels are not.

Business Hours

The following opening hours are common throughout the region.

Banks 8.30am to 2pm Monday to Friday; some also open 4pm to 7pm Thursday and 9am to 1pm Saturday

Post Offices 8.30am to 2.30pm and 4.30pm to 8pm Monday to Friday, 9.30am to 1pm Saturday

Nightclubs Midnight or 1am to 5am or 6am

Restaurants Lunch 1pm to 4pm, dinner 8.30pm to 11pm or midnight

Shops 10am to 2pm and 4.30pm to 7.30pm or 5pm to 8pm; big supermarkets and department stores generally open 10am to 10pm Monday to Saturday

Discount Cards

- The **Bilbao Bizkaia Card** (24/48/72 hours €10/15/20) entitles the user to free citywide transport, free guided tours offered by the tourist office and reductions at many sights. It can be purchased from any of the Bilbao tourist offices.

- The **San Sebastián Card** entitles users to free citywide transport, reduced admission rates at many sights, and discounts at various shops, restaurants and tour operators. Cards are valid for 10 days, cost €9 or €16 (for six or 12 trips on public transport; night trips count as two rides), and are available at the tourist office.

Electricity

Type C
220V/50Hz

Type F
230V/50Hz

Emergency

International access code	🕿 00
Country code	🕿 34
Emergencies	🕿 112

LGBTIQ+ Travellers

As in other parts of Spain, the Basque Country is generally a gay-friendly place. Homosexuality is legal, and same-sex marriage has been legal since 2005.

Bilbao hosts the region's biggest Pride (www.bilbaobizkaiapride.com) event, usually in late June.

There are a handful of gay nightspots in Bilbao and San Sebastián, as well as bars that draw a mixed crowd of gay and straight folks. For the latest listings, check out the Bilbao-focused LGBTIQ+ monthly guide Revista Blue (http://revistablue.com).

Money

The currency in Spain is the euro (€).

ATMs

ATMs are widely available in both cities, but fewer and further between on the Central Basque Coast. Many charge hefty withdrawal fees for foreign bank cards. At the time of research, Deutsche Bank and Kutxabank ATMs charged no additional fees.

Credit Cards

Credit cards are accepted in most hotels, restaurants and shops; Visa and Mastercard are the most prevalent.

Exchanging Money

Banks and building societies offer the best exchange rates; take your passport.

Tipping

Bars It's rare to leave a tip in bars (even if the bartender gives you your change on a small dish).

Restaurants Many locals leave small change, others up to 5%, which is considered generous.

Taxis Optional, but most locals round up to the nearest euro.

Money-Saving Tips

○ Many restaurants offer a lunchtime *menú del día*. These mutlicourse meals, which typically cost from €10 to €15, are a great way to eat well on a budget.

○ Selecting cash withdrawals and card payments in the local currency, when given the option, is generally better value.

Public Holidays

Many shops are closed and many attractions operate on reduced hours on the following dates:

Año Nuevo (New Year's Day) 1 January

Epifanía/Día de los Reyes Magos (Epiphany/Three Kings' Day) 6 January

Jueves Santo (Maundy/Holy Thursday) March/April

Viernes Santo (Good Friday) March/April

Fiesta del Trabajo (Labour Day) 1 May

Día de Santiago Apóstol (Feast of St James the Apostle) 25 July

La Asunción (Feast of the Assumption) 15 August

Fiesta Nacional de España (National Day) 12 October

Día de Todos los Santos (All Saints Day) 1 November

Día de la Constitución (Constitution Day) 6 December

La Inmaculada Concepción (Feast of the Immaculate Conception) 8 December

Dos & Don'ts

- Do greet people with *kaixo* ('hello' in Basque) and farewell them with *agur* (goodbye); some words of Basque are greatly appreciated.

- Alternatively, use the Spanish *hola* (hello) or *adiós* (goodbye).

- Do greet friends and family with a kiss on each cheek, or shake hands with strangers if offered.

- Don't talk politics, and definitely don't talk Basque politics unless you really know your stuff.

Navidad (Christmas) 25 December

Safe Travel

- The Basque Country is generally very safe, with few visitors experiencing any major problems.

- In Bilbao, the area just south of the old town across the river, especially on and around Calle de San Francisco, can be seedy day and night.

- Petty theft is relatively rare in the region, but stay alert for pickpockets, especially in busier areas.

- Cars, especially those belonging to tourists, are a particular target at beaches. Don't leave *anything* of value in your vehicle.

- The Basque Country is serious surf country and many beaches are plagued by dangerous undertows and large waves. Always swim in the designated swimming areas and obey lifeguards' instructions.

- ETA-related political violence is, hopefully, a thing of the past, but political protests remain common and these can occasionally turn violent. If you encounter a political protest, it's best to avoid any involvement.

- Find out the latest COVID-19 guidelines before you travel on Spain's Ministry of Health's website (www.mscbs.gob.es/en). For local requirements in the Basque Country, check www.euskadi.eus.

Toilets

- Public toilets aren't all that common in either Bilbao or San Sebastián, though some exist around the beach area and down by the port in San Sebastián.

- Another option is to use the toilets in a large shopping centre, or major train or bus station.

- If you go into a bar or restaurant to use a toilet, it's good form to buy a drink as well.

Tourist Information

Bilbao

Main Tourist Office (944 79 57 60; www.bilbaoturismo.net; Plaza Circular 1; 9am-8pm;) The very helpful main branch of the tourist office is near the Abando train station.

Tourist Office (www.bilbaoturismo.net; Alameda Mazarredo 66) Useful info point right outside the Guggenheim.

Tourist Office (☎ 944 03 14 44; www.bilbaoturismo.net; Bilbao Airport) Gives info on Bilbao and the Basque region.

San Sebastián

Oficina de Turismo (☎ 943 48 11 66; www.sansebastianturismo.com; Alameda del Boulevard 8) This friendly office offers comprehensive information on the city and the Basque Country in general.

Visas

○ Citizens or residents of EU and Schengen countries don't require a visa.

○ From 1 January 2021, non-EU nationals who don't require a visa for entry to the Schengen area need prior authorisation to enter under the new European Travel Information and Authorisation System (ETIAS; www.etias.com). Travellers can apply online; the cost is €7 for a three-year, multi-entry authorisation.

○ Nationals of other countries should check with a Spanish embassy or consulate about applying for a Schengen visa.

Language

Spanish (*español*) – often referred to as *castellano* (Castilian) to distinguish it from other languages spoken in Spain – is the most widely understood language across the country. Basque (*euskara*) is spoken in the Basque country (*el país vasco*) and is one of the four official languages of Spain. Speaking Spanish in Basque speaking cities such as Bilbao and San Sebastián will generally be expected from a foreigner. Travellers who learn a little Spanish should be relatively well understood.

Most Spanish sounds are pronounced the same as their English counterparts. Just read our pronunciation guides as if they were English and you'll be understood. Note that 'm/f' indicates masculine and feminine forms.

To enhance your trip with a phrasebook, visit lonelyplanet.com.

Basics

Hello.
Hola.   o·la

Goodbye.
Adiós.   a·dyos

How are you?
¿Qué tal?   ke tal

Fine, thanks.
Bien, gracias.   byen *gra*·thyas

Please.
Por favor.   por fa·*vor*

Thank you.
Gracias.   *gra*·thyas

Excuse me.
Perdón.   per·*don*

Sorry.
Lo siento.   lo *syen*·to

Yes./No.
Sí./No.   see/no

Do you speak (English)?
¿Habla (inglés)?   a·bla (een·*gles*)

I (don't) understand.
Yo (no) entiendo.   yo (no) en·*tyen*·do

Eating & Drinking

I'm a vegetarian. (m/f)
Soy vegetariano/a.   soy ve·khe·ta·*rya*·no/a

Cheers!
¡Salud!   sa·*loo*

That was delicious!
¡Estaba buenísimo!   es·*ta*·ba bwe·*nee*·see·mo

Please bring the bill.
Por favor nos trae la cuenta.   por fa·*vor* nos *tra*·e la *kwen*·ta

I'd like ...
Quisiera ...   kee·*sye*·ra ...

a coffee	*un café*	oon ka·fe
a table for two	*una mesa para dos*	*oo*·na me·sa pa·ra dos
a wine	*un vino*	oon vee·no
two beers	*dos cervezas*	dos ther·ve·thas

Shopping

I'd like to buy ...
Quisiera comprar ... kee·sye·ra kom·prar ...

May I look at it?
¿Puedo verlo? pwe·do ver·lo

How much is it?
¿Cuánto cuesta? kwan·to kwes·ta

That's too/very expensive.
Es muy caro. es mooy ka·ro

Emergencies

Help!
¡Socorro! so·ko·ro

Call a doctor!
¡Llame a un médico! lya·me a oon me·dee·ko

Call the police!
¡Llame a la policía! lya·me a la po·lee·thee·a

I'm lost. (m/f)
Estoy perdido/a. es·toy per·dee·do/a

I'm ill. (m/f)
Estoy enfermo/a. s·toy en·fer·mo/a

Where are the toilets?
¿Dónde están los baños? don·de es·tan los ba·nyos

Time & Numbers

What time is it?
¿Qué hora es? ke o·ra es

It's (10) o'clock.
Son (las diez). son (las dyeth)

morning mañana ma·nya·na

afternoon tarde tar·de

evening noche no·che

yesterday ayer a·yer

today hoy oy

tomorrow mañana ma·nya·na

1	uno	oo·no
2	dos	dos
3	tres	tres
4	cuatro	kwa·tro
5	cinco	theen·ko
6	seis	seys
7	siete	sye·te
8	ocho	o·cho
9	nueve	nwe·ve
10	diez	dyeth

Transport & Directions

Where's ...?
¿Dónde está ...? don·de es·ta ...

What's the address?
¿Cuál es la dirección? kwal es la dee·rek·thyon

Can you show me (on the map)?
¿Me lo puede indicar (en el mapa)? me lo pwe·de een·dee·kar (en el ma·pa)

I want to go to ...
Quisiera ir a ... kee·sye·ra eer a ...

What time does it arrive/leave?
¿A qué hora llega/sale? a ke o·ra lye·ga/sa·le

I want to get off here.
Quiero bajarme aquí. kye·ro ba·khar·me a·kee

Behind the Scenes

Send Us Your Feedback

We love to hear from travellers – your comments help make our books better. We read every word, and we guarantee that your feedback goes straight to the authors. Visit **lonelyplanet.com/contact** to submit your updates and suggestions.

Note: We may edit, reproduce and incorporate your comments in Lonely Planet products such as guidebooks, websites and digital products, so let us know if you are happy to have your name acknowledged. For a copy of our privacy policy visit lonelyplanet.com/legal.

Acknowledgements

Front cover and spine photograph: The Guggenheim Museum; Karol Kozlowski Premium RM Collection/Alamy ©
Back cover photograph: Athletic Bilbao's Estadio San Mamés; Mikolaj Barbanell / Shutterstock ©

Paul's Thanks

Muchas gracias to the Basques, ex-pats and fellow travellers who shared their passion and recommendations for this unique region of Spain: Itziar, Gabriella, Oihana, Paulo, Dean and Silvia, and in particular to Peter and Naomi Boddy. Thanks to my fellow writer Esme, and the amazing team behind the scenes, especially Sasha Drew, who took every one of my inane questions and carefully made all the pieces fit. Special thanks goes to Helena, who always manages to make the inevitable coming back home something to look forward to.

This Book

This 4th edition of Lonely Planet's Pocket *Bilbao & San Sebastián* was researched and written by Paul Stafford and Esme Fox. The previous edition was written by Catherine Le Nevez. This guidebook was produced by the following:

Commissioning Editor
Sasha Drew

Production Editor
Graham O'Neill

Cartographer
Julie Sheridan

Book Designer
Dermot Hegarty

Assisting Editors
Monique Choy,
Soo Hamilton

Cover Researcher
Hannah Blackie

Thanks to
Alex Conroy,
Melanie Dankel,
Ania Lenihan

Index

See also separate subindexes for:

- ✈ **Eating p173**
- 🍷 **Drinking p174**
- ⭐ **Entertainment p174**
- 🛍 **Shopping p175**

A

accessible travel 163
accommodation 160
activities 27
airports 33, 161-2
Aixerrota Windmill 77, 84
Albaola Foundation 153
Aquarium 9, 108-9
architecture 24, 60, 73
Arkeologi Museoa 42
arriving in Bilbao & San Sebastián 33, 161
art galleries 23, see also individual galleries
Athletic Bilbao 7, 20, 58-9
ATMs 165
Ayuntamiento 133
Azkuna Zentroa 64

B

Basílica de Santa María 80
Basílica de Santa María del Coro 113

Sights 000
Map Pages **000**

Basque Coast Geopark 100
Basque language 20, 42
Basque people, history of 79
Basquery 68
bathrooms 166
beaches 28
Bermeo 95
Biarritz Airport 33, 162
bycycle travel, see cycling
Bilbao Airport 33, 161
Bilbao, history of 66
Bilbao neigbourhoods 30-1
Bilbao New Town 53-73, 60, 62-3
 drinking 68-70
 entertainment 70-1
 food 65-8
 shopping 68-9
 sights 64-5
 walks 60-1, **60**
Bilbao Old Town 37-51, 38, 40
 drinking 47-9
 entertainment 49-50
 food 42-7
 shopping 50-1
 sights 40-1
 walks 38-9, **38**

Bilboats 64
Bilbobentura 64
boat travel 24, 25, 64, 96, 100, 115
bridges 24
budgeting 32
business hours 164
bus, travelling by 33, 162-3

C

Calle San Pedro 151-2
Camino del Norte 152
car, travelling by 163
Casa de la Historia 114
Casco Histórico 151
Castillo de Carlos V 152
Castillo de la Mota 113
Catedral de Santiago 41-2
Catedral del Buen Pastor de San Sebastián 133
cell phones 32
Central Basque Coast 91-101, 94
children, travelling with 26
climate 160
climate change 21

Concordia Train Station 61
Construcción Vacía 114
costs 32
credit cards 165
Cristóbal Balenciaga Museoa 93
Cuevas de Santimamiñe 89
currency 32
cycling 21, 87

D

Darwin Rentals 115-6
disabilities, travellers with 163-4
discount cards 164
discounts 25, 163, 164
drinking & nightlife 16-19, 38-9, see also Drinking subindex, individual neighbourhoods
driving 163

E

Ea 97
Église St-Jean Baptiste 157
El Bote 82
Elantxobe 96
electricity 164
emergencies 164

Ermita de Guadalupe 152
essential information 163
Estación de Abando 61
ETA 83
entertainment, *see also* Entertainment *subindex*, individual neighbourhoods
etiquette 166
events 48

F

festivals & events 48
food 12-15, 28, 116, *see also* Eating *subindex*/individual neighbourhoods Michelin Stars 13
football 58
Foster, Sir Norman 73
free attractions 25
Fuente del Perro 42
Funicular de Artxanda 65
funicular railway (Monte Igueldo) 126

G

Galerías de Punta Begoña 81
gay travellers 164
Gehry, Frank 57
geology 100
Gernika 7, 88-9
Getaria 7, 92-3

Sights 000
Map Pages **000**

Getxo 75-87, **76, 78-9**
drinking 85-6
food 82-5
shopping 87
sights 80-2
walks 76-7, **76**
Grande Plage 157

H

Hendaye 155
highlights 6-11
hiking 84, 143
history 43
holidays 165
Hondarribia 149-55, **150**
drinking 155
food 152-4
shopping p155
sights 151-2
Hotel Maria Cristina 132

I

Iglesia de San Salvador 93
Iglesia de San Vicente 114
Iglesia San Nicolás de Bari 41
internet resources 32, 160
Isla de San Nicolás 98
Isla de Santa Clara 115
itineraries 30-1
Itsasmuseum 61, 64

J

Jardines Albia 61
Jardines de Miramar 132

K

kayaking 25, 64, 96, 115

Koldo Mitxelena Kulturunea 132

L

languages 32, 42, 168
Las Siete Calles 41
lauburu, 43
Lekeitio 97-8
Les Halles Centrales 157
lesbian travellers 164-5
LGBTIQ+ travellers 164-5
live music 17

M

Maison Adam 157
Maison de l'Infante 157
Maison Louis XIV 157
Mercado de la Ribera 50
metro, travel 33, 73, 162
Michelin stars 13
mobile phones 32
money 32, 165
Monte Igueldo 11, 122-39, **128, 130-1**
drinking 135-8
entertainment 138
food 133-5
shopping 138-9
sights 132-3
walks 128-9, **128**
Monte Urgull 113
Mundaka 96
Museo de Bellas Artes 61, 70
Museo de Euskal Herria 89
Museo de la Paz de Gernika 89

Museo Guggenheim Bilbao 6, 8, 54-5
Museo Marítimo Vasco 114
Museum of the Basque Country 89
museums 23, see also individual museums
music 16
Mutriku 99

N

nightlife 16, *see* drinking & nightlife, Drinking *subindex*

O

opening hours 164

P

Palacio Miramar 133
paragliding 84
parks & gardens, *see* individual parks
Parque de Alderdi Eder 133
Parque de Cristina Enea 143
Parque de Doña Casilda de Iturrizar 61
Parque de los Pueblos de Europa 89
Parque Usategi 77
Pasaia 143, 149-55, **150**
drinking 155
food 152-4
shopping p155
sights 151-2
Paseo de las Grandes Villas 81
pintxos 12-15, 44, 110-11, 145
planning 32

Playa de Arrigunaga 77
Playa de Ereaga 82
Playa de Hondarribia 151
Playa de la Concha 10
Playa de la Zurriola 143
Playa de Ondarreta 132
Plaza de Gipuzkoa 132
Plaza de la Constitución 115
Plaza del Solar 80
Plaza de San Nicolás 77
Portugalete 75-87, **76, 78-9**
 drinking 85-6
 food 82-5
 shopping 87
 sights 80-2
 walks 76-7, **76**
public holidays 165
Puente Colgante 80
Puente de Maria Cristina 133
Puente Zubizuri 61
Pukas Surf Eskola 143
Punta Galea 84

R

responsible travel 20-1
Rialia Museo de la Industría 80-1

S

safety 166
San Nicolás de Bari 77

San Sebastián Airport 33, 161
San Sebastián Gros 141-7, **142**
 drinking 146
 entertainment 146-7
 food 143-6
 shopping 147
 sights 143
San Sebastián New Town 122-39, **128, 130-1**
 drinking 135-8
 entertainment 138
 food 133-5
 shopping 138-9
 sights 132-3
 walks 128-9, **128**
San Sebastián neighbourhoods 100-1
San Sebastián Parte Vieja 104-21, **110, 112**
 drinking 118-9
 entertainment 119-20
 food 116-19
 shopping 120-1
 sights 113-15
 walks 110-11, **110**
San Telmo Museoa 106-7
Sede de Sanidad del Gobierno Vasco 61
shopping 22, see also Shopping subindex, individual neighbourhoods
sports 27, 96, 98, 101
St-Jean-de-Luz, France 156
surfing 27, 96, 100-1, 121, 143

T

Tabakalera 146
taxi, travelling by 163
Teatro Campos Elíseos 61
theatres 17
time 32
tipping 32, 165
toilets 166
Torre Iberdrola 61
tourist information 160, 166
tours 27, 49-50, 59, 81, 89, 157, 164
 boat 24, 25, 64, 96, 100
 food 138-9
Tower of Monte Igueldo 127
trains, travelling by 162
tram, travelling by 33, 163
transport 33
travel card 163
txakoli 18-19
txikiteros singers 46
Txomin Taberna 77

U

Universidad de Deusto 72
Urdaibai Bird Center 89
useful websites 160

V

visas 32, 167

W

walking 27, see hiking, see also individual neighbourhoods
weather 160
websites 32
wine 96

Z

Zarautz 100-1
Zubizuri 64-5
Zumaia 99-100

✖ Eating

A

Alabama Café 145
Alameda 154-5
Altuna 134
Amelia 134
Antonio Bar 133
Arnoldo Heladeria 134
Astelena 117

B

Bacaicoa Taberna 46
Bar Borda Berri 116
Bar Charly 44-5
Bascook 67
Baster 43-4
Bergara Bar 144
Berton 46
Bodega Donostiarra 144
Bodegón Alejandro 116
Brasserie Igeretxe 85

C

Café de la Concha 134-5
Casa Rufo 67
Casa Urola 116
Casa Valles 135
Casa Victor Montes 42-3
Claudio: La Feria del Jamón 45

E

El Globo 66
El Huevo Frito 67-8
El Puertito 67
El Txoko Berria 46-7

G

Gastroteka Danontzat 152
Gerald's Bar 144-5
Gran Sol 154
Gure Toki 43

I

Irrintzi 43

J

Jai Alai 82

K

Karola Etxea 82
Kata.4 135
Kofradia 117-18

L

La Camelia 68
La Hermandad de Pescadores 154
La Kazuela 84
La Txuleteria 145
La Viña del Ensanche 65-6
Laía Erretegia 152-4
Los Fueros 47

M

Mapa Verde 145-6

Sights 000
Map Pages **000**

N

Nerua Guggenheim Bilbao 67

P

Punta Malabata 84

R

Restaurante Kokotxa 116
Restaurante Muxumartin 117
Restaurante Tenis Ondarreta 135
Rio-Oja 45
Rojo y Negro 135

S

Satistegi 84-5
Singular 68

T

Tamarises Izarra 82-4
Txepetxa 116
Txuleta 117

X

Xarma 143-4

Y

Yandiola 67

Z

Zortziko 66

🍸 Drinking

A

Amona Margarita 155
Arkaitzpe 119

B

Baobab 69
Bar Arrantzale 85
Bataplan Disco 135
Be Club 119
Bohemian Lane 49
Botanika 136-7

C

Café Iruña 69
Casa Vicente 86
Charamel 49
Cinnamon 70
Cork 68
Côte Bar 118
Cotton Club 69

E

El Balcón de la Lola 69
El Paladar 86

G

Garua 119
Gin Fizz 68-9
Gu 136

H

Hells Bells 49
Hole Pub 119

K

Koh Tao 137

L

La Gintonería Donostiarra 146
La Mera Mera 138
La Peña Athletic 47

M

Mala Gissona Beer House 146
Museo del Whisky 136

O

Old Town Coffee 136
Ondarra 146

P

Pokhara 136
Portu Zaharra Bar 86

R

Residence 69

V

Vinoteka Ardoka 155

✪ Entertainment

A

Altxerri Jazz Bar 120

B

Back & Stage 71
Bilborock 71

D

Doka 138

E

Etxekalte 120
Euskalduna Palace 70-1

K

Kafe Antzokia 70
Kursaal 146

L

Le Bukowski 147

T

Teatro Arriaga 49-50
Teatro Campos Elíseos 70
Teatro Principal 119-20
Teatro Victoria Eugenia 138

🛍 Shopping

A

Aitor Lasa 121
Alboka Artesanía 121
Almacen Coloniales y Bacalao Gregorio Martín 51
Ana Valladares 87
Arrese 51
Ätakontu 50

B

Beltza 121

C

Casa Ponsol 120-1
Chocolates de Mendaro 72, 139
Conservas Hondarribia 155
Crosta Ogitegia-Enkarterri Concept Store 72-3

D

DendAZ 71

E

Elkano 1 Gaztagune 139
Erviti 139

G

Goiuri 139
Gorostiaga 50

L

La Granja Selección 87
La Oka 72
La Quesaría 50
Lauter 147
Le Chocolat 51
Loreak Mendian 139
Lukas Gourmet Shop 138-9

M

Market 73

Mercado de la Bretxa 121
Mercado San Martín 139
Mika Kids Concept Store 87

O

Orriak 51

P

Peletería Ramón Ezkerra 50
Perfumería Benegas 138
Persuade 73
Power Records 72

R

Room 278 121
Rzik 51

S

soule. 147

Z

Zubiarte 73

Our Writers

Paul Stafford

Paul is based in Birmingham, UK, but can usually be found anywhere that is not at all like Birmingham. He has lived in five countries, including a balmy stint in Sevilla, Spain. San Sebastián is a place that captivated him so much when he first visited in 2007 that he feels compelled to visit at least once every few years. When not entangled in a web of words and pictures, he is making and releasing music as one half of the rock duo First Frontier.

Esme Fox

Esme left her home country of England when she was 12 and has since lived on five different continents and many different countries, while travelling to even more. For the past eight years, she has mainly been based in one of her favourite countries – Spain. She lives in Barcelona, but travels often to the Basque Country. She was in Bilbao for the 20th anniversary of the Guggenheim in 2017 and was there again for its 25th in 2022, while researching for this guide. Esme has been a professional travel writer for over 10 years and has written many guidebooks and countless articles about Spain and other countries around the world, several of them for Lonely Planet.

Published by Lonely Planet Global Limited
CRN 554153
4th edition – Jun 2023
ISBN 978 1 83869 177 6
© Lonely Planet 2023   Photographs © as indicated 2023
10 9 8 7 6 5 4 3 2
Printed in Malaysia

Although the authors and Lonely Planet have taken all reasonable care in preparing this book, we make no warranty about the accuracy or completeness of its content and, to the maximum extent permitted, disclaim all liability arising from its use.

All rights reserved. No part of this publication may be copied, stored in a retrieval system, or transmitted in any form by any means, electronic, mechanical, recording or otherwise, except brief extracts for the purpose of review, and no part of this publication may be sold or hired, without the written permission of the publisher. Lonely Planet and the Lonely Planet logo are trademarks of Lonely Planet and are registered in the US Patent and Trademark Office and in other countries. Lonely Planet does not allow its name or logo to be appropriated by commercial establishments, such as retailers, restaurants or hotels. Please let us know of any misuses: lonelyplanet.com/legal/intellectual-property.

a simple guide to
blood pressure

BESTMEDICINE Health Handbooks

A Simple Guide to Blood Pressure
First published – September 2005

Published by
CSF Medical Communications Ltd
1 Bankside, Lodge Road, Long Hanborough
Oxfordshire, OX29 8LJ, UK
T +44 (0)1993 885370 F +44 (0)1993 881868
enquiries@bestmedicine.com
www.bestmedicine.com
www.csfmedical.com

Editor Dr Eleanor Bull
Medical Editor Professor Bryan Williams
Contributing Editor Dr Jonathan Morrell
Contributing Author Dr Scott Chambers
Creative Director & Project Manager Julia Potterton
Designer Lee Smith
Layout Julie Smith
Publisher Stephen I'Anson

© CSF Medical Communications Ltd 2005

All rights reserved

ISBN: 1-905466-04-8

BESTMEDICINE is a trademark of CSF Medical Communications Ltd

This *BESTMEDICINE Health Handbook* is provided for general information only, and should not be treated as a substitute for the medical advice of your own doctor or any other healthcare professional. You are strongly urged to consult your doctor before taking, stopping or changing any of the products referred to in this book or any other medication that has been prescribed or recommended by your doctor, and before stopping, changing or commencing any alternative treatment or lifestyle measure referred to. Whilst every effort has been made to ensure the accuracy of the information at the date of publication CSF Medical Communications Ltd and The Patients Association accept no responsibility for any errors or omissions or for any consequences arising from anything included in or excluded from this *BESTMEDICINE Health Handbook* nor for the contents of any external internet site or other information source listed and do not endorse any commercial product or service mentioned.

contents

What happens normally?	1
The basics	9
Why me?	27
Simple science	47
Managing blood pressure	61
Simple extras	109

ACKNOWLEDGEMENTS

The *BESTMEDICINE Simple Guides* team is very grateful to a number of people who have made this project possible. In particular we'd like to thank Anne Taylor, Jane Cassidy, Caroline Delasalle and Amelie (5 months). Thank you to Ben for his endless enthusiasm, energy and creativity, to Molly (7) and George (5) and of course to Hetta. Julie and Rob who went far beyond the call of duty and Julie's ability to put pages together for hours on end was hugely inspiring.

A Simple Guide to your Health Service

Emma Catherall   Co-ordinator

Advisory Panel

Richard Stevens	GP
Anne Taylor	Practice nurse
Michael Schachter	Hospital specialist
Michael Gum	Pharmacist
John Chater	Binley's health and care information specialist *www.binleys.com*

simple

simple *adj*. **1.** easy to understand or do: *a simple problem*. **2.** plain; unadorned: *a simple dress*. **3.** Not combined or complex: *a simple mechanism*. **4.** Unaffected or unpretentious: *although he became famous he remained a simple man*. **5.** sincere; frank: *a simple explanation was readily accepted*. **6.** (*prenominal*) without additions or modifications: *the witness told the simple truth*.

ABOUT THE AUTHOR

ANNA PALMER

Anna Palmer graduated from Cardiff University with a BSc Honours degree in Biochemistry before completing a PhD in Physiology at St Thomas' Hospital, London. Anna then spent 5 years researching in the field of cardiovascular disease. In her spare time, Anna belongs to a skydiving team who regularly hone their flying skills over the Oxfordshire skies.

ABOUT THE EDITOR

BRYAN WILLIAMS

Bryan Williams is a consultant physician and Professor of Medicine at the University of Leicester. He is a past president of the British Hypertension Society (2001–2003) and is currently Chairman of its information service and national hypertension guidelines working party.

FOREWORD

TRISHA MACNAIR
Doctor and BBC Health Journalist

Getting involved in managing your own medical condition – or helping those you love or care for to manage theirs – is a vital step towards keeping as healthy as possible. Whilst doctors, nurses and the rest of your healthcare team can help you with expert advice and guidance, nobody knows your body, your symptoms and what is right for *you* as well as you do.

There is no long-term (chronic) medical condition or illness that I can think of where the person concerned has absolutely no influence at all on their situation. The way you choose to live your life, from the food you eat to the exercise you take, will impact upon your disease, your well-being and how able you are to cope. You are in charge!

Being involved in making choices about your treatment helps you to feel in control of your problems, and makes sure you get the help that you really need. Research clearly shows that when people living with a chronic illness take an active role in looking after themselves, they can bring about significant improvements in their illness and vastly improve the quality of life they enjoy. Of course, there may be occasions when you feel particularly unwell and it all seems out of your control. Yet most of the time there are plenty of things that you can do in order to reduce the negative effects that your condition can have on your life. This way you feel as good as possible and may even be able to alter the course of your condition.

So how do you gain the confidence and skills to take an active part in managing your condition, communicate with health professionals, and work through sometimes worrying and emotive issues? The answer is to become better informed. Reading about your problem, talking to others who have been through similar experiences, and hearing what the experts have to say will all help to build-up your understanding and help you to take an active role in your own health care.

BESTMEDICINE Simple Guides provide an invaluable source of help, giving you the facts that you need in order to understand the key issues and discuss them with your doctors and other professionals involved in your care. The information is presented in an accessible way but without neglecting the important details. Produced independently and under the guidance of medical experts *A Simple Guide to Blood Pressure* is an evidence-based, balanced and up-to-date review that I hope you will find enables you to play an active part in the successful management of your condition.

what happens normally?

WHAT HAPPENS NORMALLY?

In order to understand what's going on when you have high blood pressure, it is important to first understand what happens in your body under normal circumstances.

YOUR CIRCULATORY SYSTEM

An adult's circulatory system is over 60,000 miles long. That's long enough to stretch around the world more than twice!

Your circulatory system consists of your heart and the network of arteries and veins that carry your blood. Arteries carry oxygen-rich blood away from the heart. Veins carry deoxygenated blood (from which the oxygen has been removed) back to the heart. You could consider your circulation as being akin to the road network in the UK, with the motorways and major roads representing the arteries and veins, and the minor roads representing the small blood vessels that feed our organs with blood. Like the road network, blood flow around our circulation can become disrupted and pressure can build up in the system.

Did you know that your heart beats over 100,000 times a day?

The heart is a highly muscular organ and is responsible for pumping blood around your body. The heart beats continuously, never pausing to rest, and ensures a continuous supply of oxygen, nutrients and other vital substances to every part of our body, allowing us to function optimally whether we are fast asleep or running a marathon.

what happens normally?

The heart is made up of four chambers which are enclosed by layers of muscle. These four chambers are called the left and right atria (singular atrium) and the left and right ventricles. During a single heart beat, the muscle of the heart contracts and the walls of these chambers are pulled in like a squeezed fist. This exerts pressure on the blood within the chambers of the heart. It is this force which pushes the blood from the atria into the ventricles and then from the ventricles out into the circulation. This simple pumping action and the resistance to it in the closed system of our circulation is what creates 'blood pressure'.

The force your heart uses to pump blood around your body is roughly equivalent to giving a tennis ball a good, hard squeeze.

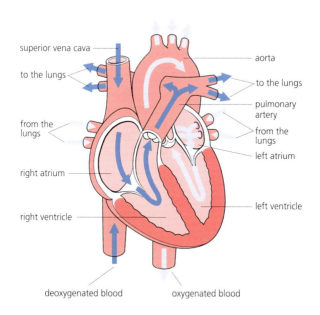

For simplicity, the movement of blood around our bodies can be split into a number of key stages.

1 Oxygen is transferred from the air into our bloodstream by our lungs. This oxygen-rich blood is said to be 'oxygenated'.

2 Oxygenated blood passes into the left atrium of the heart which squeezes (contracts) and pushes the blood into the left ventricle. The left ventricle – the largest and most powerful chamber of the heart – has the job of pumping the oxygenated blood hard enough to reach every part of our body. It does this via the aorta (the largest artery in the body).

3 Blood pressure in the aorta is at its highest to ensure that oxygen and other vital nutrients (like sugars, fats and vitamins) are delivered to the parts of the body that require them.

4 The tissues and organs of the body take up the oxygen from the blood and replace it with the waste product, carbon dioxide.

what happens normally?

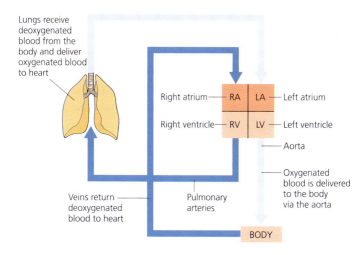

5. The blood is now said to be 'deoxygenated' and is returned to the right atrium of the heart via the veins.

6. The right atrium squeezes to pass the deoxygenated blood into the right ventricle which then pumps it back to the lungs where it can be replenished with fresh oxygen.

7. The process starts again.

a simple guide to blood pressure

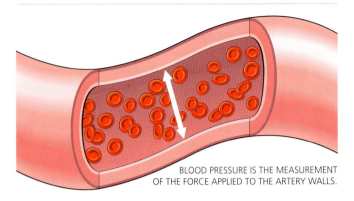

BLOOD PRESSURE IS THE MEASUREMENT OF THE FORCE APPLIED TO THE ARTERY WALLS.

WHAT IS BLOOD PRESSURE?

Blood pressure is the force (or push) of your blood on the walls of your arteries as it is pumped from your heart around the body. By way of analogy, consider your own domestic water supply. If your supply is disrupted and you have 'low water pressure' then you find the water slows to just a trickle. Blood pressure is important because, without it, our blood wouldn't flow at all.

You may have had your blood pressure measured as part of a routine check on your general health. Most people will have their

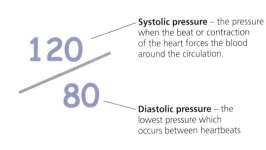

Systolic pressure – the pressure when the beat or contraction of the heart forces the blood around the circulation.

Diastolic pressure – the lowest pressure which occurs between heartbeats

blood pressure measured at some point in their lives. Your blood pressure measurement will take the form of two numbers, which denote your systolic (*sis-TOL-ick*) and diastolic (*die-ass-TOL-ick*) blood pressure (e.g. 120/80 or 'one twenty over eighty'). The top number, which is the systolic pressure, represents the pressure in your arteries when your heart is forcing blood through them. The bottom number, the diastolic pressure, is the pressure in your arteries when your heart relaxes between beats. These numbers are presented in units of millimetres of mercury (or mmHg, Hg being the chemical symbol for mercury). This reflects the way in which blood pressure has been measured ever since it was first 'discovered'.

the basics

HIGH BLOOD PRESSURE – THE BASICS

High blood pressure occurs when your blood exerts a persistent and abnormally high pressure, or force, on your circulatory system.

HOW HIGH IS HIGH?

High blood pressure – or hypertension – is generally defined as a systolic blood pressure of greater than 140 mmHg and a diastolic blood pressure of greater than 90 mmHg.

WHY IS HAVING HIGH BLOOD PRESSURE A PROBLEM?

Our blood pressure naturally fluctuates throughout the day. Blood pressure only presents a problem when it is persistently high. This is because it puts both your circulatory system and the organs it supplies with blood (including the heart and the brain), under too great a strain.

If high blood pressure is not controlled properly, it can lead to a number of serious complications and cardiovascular diseases (CVD) including:

- angina and heart attacks
- strokes and 'mini' strokes
- heart failure
- kidney damage
- eye problems.

A heart attack occurs when the heart's own supply of oxygenated blood is cut off by a blockage in one of the vessels that supply it – the coronary arteries.

the basics

Persistently high blood pressure has also been implicated in other problems with the circulation such as peripheral arterial disease (disease of the arteries in the extremities of the body, including the legs), intermittent claudication (pain in the limbs when you walk), aortic aneurysm (a dangerous ballooning of the aorta – the main artery leaving the heart), and even the development of brain disorders such as dementia.

There are many ways that you, working closely with your doctor and nurse, can bring your blood pressure under control and significantly reduce your risk of developing these complications. We'll talk about the different ways you can keep your blood pressure under control in this *Simple Guide*.

Heart failure occurs when your heart does not pump blood around the body as well as it should.

SYMPTOMS

High blood pressure rarely has any symptoms and the only way of knowing if you have it is to have your blood pressure measured. Therefore, and as recommended in guidelines issued by the British Hypertension Society, it is advisable that you have your blood pressure measured at least every 5 years, and preferably more frequently if at all possible.

If your blood pressure is not controlled and becomes extremely high (a situation known as **severe** or **malignant hypertension**) then it is possible that you may experience symptoms including:

- dizziness
- blurred vision
- headaches
- confusion
- sleepiness
- breathlessness.

However, these instances are rare and affect less than 1% of people with high blood pressure. Where blood pressure remains persistently and severely elevated, it may be necessary for your GP to refer you to a hypertension specialist in hospital.

HIGH BLOOD PRESSURE MYTHS

- A red face or feeling flushed does not mean you have high blood pressure.
- Having high blood pressure does not mean you will be tense, nervous or hyperactive.
- Nosebleeds are hardly ever an indicator of high blood pressure.

If you are not experiencing any symptoms of high blood pressure, this doesn't mean that your high blood pressure is not causing damage to your circulatory system. It can still lead to heart disease, stroke and the other complications described previously. This is why high blood pressure is sometimes referred to as the 'silent killer'. Try not to be too alarmed by this label. The good news is that high blood pressure is relatively easy-to-treat.

HIGH BLOOD PRESSURE IS SOMETMES REFERRED TO AS THE 'SILENT KILLER'.

TYPES OF HIGH BLOOD PRESSURE

There are two main types of high blood pressure.

■ **Essential (primary) hypertension**
This accounts for the majority of cases of high blood pressure – about 95%. The specific cause of essential hypertension is unknown, although it is likely to be related to a combination of lifestyle factors including inactivity and diet.

■ **Secondary hypertension**
This type of high blood pressure is much less common and only accounts for about 5% of cases of high blood pressure. The high blood pressure characteristic of secondary hypertension is a consequence of an underlying medical condition (e.g. kidney disease) or a reaction to certain drugs (e.g. the contraceptive pill).

RISK FACTORS FOR HIGH BLOOD PRESSURE

In the majority of cases, we don't know what causes high blood pressure. This is particularly true of essential hypertension. There are, however, several risk factors which can make you more likely to develop high blood pressure. These include:

- being overweight
- not exercising enough
- having too much salt in your diet
- not eating enough fresh fruit and vegetables
- drinking too much alcohol.

Although smoking only appears to cause transient increases in blood pressure, it dramatically increases your chances of developing heart disease or having a stroke. Therefore, anyone who smokes should make a real effort to stop, and your doctor and nurse will be able to offer you advice to help you to quit.

the basics

Whilst eating too much fat (especially saturated fats found in meat and dairy products) is not directly related to increases in blood pressure, it is a risk factor for cardiovascular disease as it is associated with high levels of cholesterol in the blood. Consequently, you should make a real effort to reduce the amount of saturated fat in your diet. By reducing the amount of fat you consume, you will also be making great strides towards reducing your weight, which is another risk factor for developing high blood pressure.

EATING TOO MUCH FAT CAN INCREASE YOUR RISK OF CARDIOVASCULAR DISEASE.

Luckily, the 'modifiable' risk factors described above can be reduced by making relatively simple changes to your lifestyle. However, there are other factors which influence blood pressure that are beyond our control. These include:

- old age (blood pressure has a tendency to rise as we get older)
- a family history of high blood pressure (we are more likely to have high blood pressure if both our parents have it)
- ethnicity (high blood pressure is more common in black people)
- gender (high blood pressure is slightly more common in men than in women).

High blood pressure can sometimes have specific causes. For instance, secondary hypertension usually occurs as a result of having another disorder (like kidney disease or disorders of the adrenal glands), or as a consequence of taking other medications (e.g. the combined oral contraceptive pill or steroids). Blood pressure can also rise during pregnancy, and in stressful situations. 'White coat hypertension' is a good example of this. This refers to a situation where someone's blood pressure is raised when they are at the doctor's surgery or in hospital, but remains normal for the rest of the time. White coat hypertension may be confirmed or ruled out by measuring your own blood pressure at home. Your GP, nurse or pharmacist will be able to offer you advice about this and the home blood pressure-monitoring machines that are available.

WHITE COAT HYPERTENSION DESCRIBES RAISED BLOOD PRESSURE UNDER STRESSFUL SITUATIONS.

a simple guide to blood pressure

DIAGNOSING HIGH BLOOD PRESSURE

Sphygmomanometer derives from 'sphygmo', meaning pulse or pulsation, and 'manometer' which is a pressure gauge for gases and liquids.

Your blood pressure will be measured using a sphygmomanometer or 'sphyg'. The traditional mercury sphygs are rapidly being replaced by automated devices with a dial or digital read-out.

A blood pressure reading depends on a number of factors, including:

- whether you have recently exercised
- how stressed you are
- whether you are standing or sitting
- the time of day.

WHY IS MERCURY USED IN BLOOD PRESSURE MEASUREMENT?

- Although a metal, mercury is a liquid at room temperature. This makes it ideal for blood pressure measurement.
- When you put pressure on a column of mercury, it moves; the greater the pressure the further it moves. The distance (in millimetres [mm]) by which a column of mercury can be raised in a glass tube has been used for decades to measure blood pressure. The chemical symbol for mercury is Hg. So, for example, you may see blood pressure written as 140/80 mmHg.
- Although the mercury in a sphyg is safely encased in a closed system, we know that mercury is a toxic heavy metal and we should do everything that we can to reduce the risk of human contact or of it being released into the environment.

This is why it is important to have your blood pressure measured in a controlled environment by a qualified healthcare professional. If your blood pressure is greater than 140/90 mmHg then your blood pressure is too high. However, this diagnosis will not be made on the basis of a single measurement. Your doctor or nurse will measure your blood pressure at least twice, often at the beginning and at the end of a consultation. If your blood pressure is high you will then be asked to make another appointment to have it checked again. Only when your blood pressure reading is routinely high will a definitive diagnosis of hypertension be made.

Even though aneroid sphygs use air rather than mercury, blood pressure measurement is still translated into millimetres of mercury. This is shortened to mmHg.

YOUR DOCTOR MAY PERFORM OTHER TESTS

Your doctor may want to perform the following additional tests to rule out other potentially serious diseases, such as cardiovascular disease, heart failure, kidney disease and eye problems:

- blood test
- urine test
- physical examination
- electrocardiogram (ECG).

In an effort to determine your future risk of cardiovascular complications, your doctor is also likely to ask you additional questions such as:

- are you a smoker and how much do you smoke?
- how much alcohol do you drink each week?
- is there a history of high blood pressure in your family?
- have you or anyone in your family ever suffered with any heart problems or diabetes?
- do you engage in regular exercise?

From the answers you give to these questions and the results of your blood tests, your doctor will be able to calculate your 'cardiovascular risk'. This is a measure of how high your risk is of having a heart attack or suffering a stroke, and this risk is usually specified as a percentage over a fixed period of time, usually 10 years.

KNOWING YOUR NUMBERS

Ask your doctor or nurse to write down your blood pressure reading for you and then you can check it against your next reading. In this way you will be playing an active role in managing your blood pressure.

The Blood Pressure Association in the UK (*www.bpassoc.org.uk*) are currently running a campaign to highlight the importance of knowing your blood pressure numbers.

Only one-quarter of people with high blood pressure know what their blood pressure reading is.

Cardiovascular risk is calculated for two reasons:

1. to determine whether a person with mild hypertension requires treatment
2. to determine whether a person may benefit from extra (complementary) risk-reducing strategies (i.e. treatment with aspirin and/or statins [cholesterol-lowering drugs]).

Try our online cardiovascular risk calculator
www.bestmedicine.com

The World Health Organization has acknowledged that high blood pressure is the most important preventable cause of death and illness worldwide.

MANAGING HIGH BLOOD PRESSURE

The British Hypertension Society has produced detailed guidance for doctors and nurses to help them to treat (or manage) high blood pressure effectively.

In general, if your blood pressure is too high and your doctor diagnoses you with hypertension, it is likely that they will first give you lifestyle advice. You will be offered a further appointment to come back and have your blood pressure measured again. Only once your doctor has confirmed that you have consistently high blood pressure, which has not responded to the lifestyle changes you have made, are you likely to be prescribed drugs that lower your blood pressure.

WHAT SHOULD BE MY TARGET BLOOD PRESSURE?

In the UK, the current blood pressure target as set out by the British Hypertension Society is less than 140/85 mmHg.

If you have diabetes then your blood pressure target level is even lower and currently stands at 130/80 mmHg.

If your cardiovascular risk is judged to be high, your doctor may also prescribe you other drugs, such as aspirin and statins (cholesterol-lowering drugs), as well as blood pressure-lowering drugs.

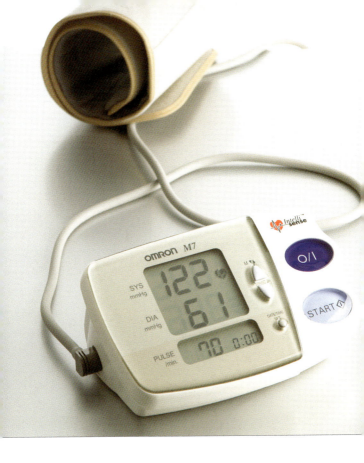

BLOOD PRESSURE MONITORING

If you are diagnosed with hypertension your doctor will ask you to make an appointment to have your blood pressure checked at regular intervals. Some patients may also opt to purchase a blood pressure monitoring device (available from most high street pharmacies) and keep track of their blood pressure themselves. The British Hypertension Society has produced some guidance on which machines are accurate and suitable for use in the home (*www.bhsoc.org*).

LIFESTYLE CHANGES TO REDUCE BLOOD PRESSURE

By ensuring that we keep our weight down, take more exercise, drink less alcohol and improve our diet, we can make great strides towards keeping our blood pressure at a safe level.

- Reduce your salt intake to less than 6 grams each day (about a teaspoon). Beware, many processed foods contain large amounts of salt.
- Limit your alcohol intake to no more than 21 units per week (men) or 14 units per week (women).
- Engage in at least 30 minutes of aerobic exercise (e.g. brisk walking) on most days of the week.
- Eat at least five portions of fresh fruit and vegetables every day.

BLOOD PRESSURE-LOWERING DRUGS

By working in partnership with your doctor you should be able to settle on the drugs that keep your blood pressure controlled without causing you unwelcome side-effects and unnecessary inconvenience. Remember that the lifestyle advice mentioned previously still applies when you are prescribed a blood pressure-lowering drug.

Antihypertensives can be divided into different categories (or classes) according to the different ways in which they work in the body. Whilst there are additional classes of drug that your doctor may prescribe under certain special circumstances, the main ones are listed below.

- Diuretics (e.g. bendroflumethiazide [Aprinox®], chlortalidone [Hygroton®])
  – Lower blood pressure by acting on the kidneys, causing them to eliminate excessive salt in the blood through the urine. This reduces the volume of the liquid in your circulation and thereby lowers your blood pressure.
- Alpha-blockers (e.g. doxazosin [Cardura®], terazosin [Hytrin®])
  – Lower blood pressure by blocking receptors in the muscles that line our blood vessels. When the receptors are blocked, the blood vessels open up (dilate), blood flows more freely and blood pressure is reduced.
- Beta-blockers (e.g. atenolol [Tenormin®], bisoprolol [Emcor®])
  – Lower blood pressure by slowing down the heart and reducing the force of its contractions, thereby reducing the

Drugs that lower blood pressure are also known as antihypertensives.

pressure exerted by its pumping action. Beta-blockers also open up (dilate) the blood vessels by altering the production of a hormone called renin, which reduces the resistance in the system and makes it easier for the heart to work.

- Calcium-channel blockers (e.g. amlodipine [Istin®], felodipine [Plendil®])
  - Lower blood pressure by blocking the entry of calcium into cells. When calcium enters muscle cells, for example, they contract. By inhibiting the contraction of muscles that line our blood vessels, the vessels open up thereby making blood flow easier and reducing blood pressure.
- Angiotensin-converting enzyme (ACE) inhibitors (e.g. perindopril [Coversyl®], ramipril [Tritace®])
  - Lower blood pressure by blocking the production of a hormone called angiotensin II, which is involved in constricting blood vessels. In this way, they open up the blood vessels and so reduce blood pressure.
- Angiotensin receptor blockers (ARBs) (e.g. losartan [Cozaar®], irbesartan [Aprovel®])
  - Work in a similar way to ACE inhibitors by blocking the constrictive effects of angiotensin II. In contrast to the ACE inhibitors, they do this by blocking the binding of the angiotensin to specific receptors rather than by reducing its production. Because angiotensin cannot constrict the blood vessels the vessels open up (dilate) and pressure in the system is reduced.

why me?

a simple guide to blood pressure

WHY ME?

If you, or a member of your family, have recently been diagnosed with high blood pressure, you're not alone. High blood pressure affects nearly 1 billion people worldwide.

HOW COMMON IS HIGH BLOOD PRESSURE?

Worldwide, nearly 1 billion people – or roughly one-quarter of the total adult population – have high blood pressure. This figure is set to increase. In the UK, high blood pressure is thought to affect more than 16 million people. In England alone, 34% of men and 30% of women have raised blood pressure (above 140/90 mmHg) or are being treated for high blood pressure. In the older population, high blood pressure is even more common and affects more than half of those who are over the age of 60.

By 2025, the number of people with high blood pressure is expected to reach almost 1.6 billion.

WHY IS HIGH BLOOD PRESSURE BECOMING MORE COMMON?

High blood pressure is often described in the media as a 'disease of affluence'. This suggests that it affects only those people who can afford an extravagant lifestyle. This is misleading since hypertension, and cardiovascular disease in general, are becoming more and more common in developing countries.

It is more likely that global lifestyle changes have a greater role to play in the increasing incidence of hypertension. The increased availability of convenience foods has led to a decline in the consumption of fresh vegetables and whole grains, and an increased intake of salt, fats and sugars, and calories in general. These gradual shifts have been accompanied by reduced levels of physical activity and have resulted in an increasingly overweight and diabetes-prone population.

Increased alcohol consumption has helped to fuel global increases in blood pressure.

The fact that there is so much more awareness amongst healthcare professionals regarding the importance of high blood pressure means that the detection of high blood pressure has increased. In addition, as our knowledge of the importance of hypertension as a risk factor for cardiovascular disease has grown, blood pressure targets have become even lower. This has meant that many more people, who were not previously considered to have high blood pressure, now receive this diagnosis.

WHO GETS HIGH BLOOD PRESSURE?

High blood pressure can affect anyone and everyone. In younger people, hypertension tends to take the form of a high diastolic blood pressure (the bottom number of the two blood pressure figures) whereas older people tend to develop a high systolic blood pressure (the higher number).

There are certain groups of people who are more at risk of developing high blood pressure.

- High blood pressure is particularly common in people over the age of 60, as blood pressure has a natural tendency to rise with age.
- High blood pressure is especially prevalent in black people, and occurs about three times more frequently in this group than in white people. This difference arises because of genetic differences between the two populations.
- High blood pressure appears to run in families, so if both your parents have high

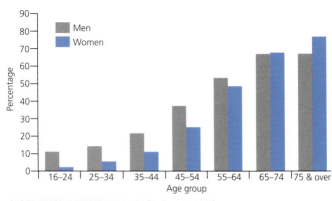

BLOOD PRESSURE RISES WITH AGE (ENGLAND, 2003).

why me?

blood pressure, you too are also more likely to develop it.
- High blood pressure is very common amongst people with diabetes or kidney disease, mainly because the kidney plays a critical role in blood pressure control.
- High blood pressure can occur when you are pregnant or as a side-effect of some types of drugs (e.g. the combined oral contraceptive pill).

WHY IS MY BLOOD PRESSURE HIGH?

There are a number of different reasons why you may have developed high blood pressure.

Age and high blood pressure

Our blood pressure has a natural tendency to rise as we get older. In the UK, the prevalence of high blood pressure amongst middle-aged people is about 20% but this rises to over 50% in people aged over 60. High blood pressure also occurs in younger people but its prevalence is low (less than 20%).

High blood pressure runs in the family

If both of your parents have high blood pressure, then there is a greater chance that you will have it too. Studies have confirmed that a child's blood pressure is more closely related to that of its parents if the child is related by blood rather than if the child is adopted. This shows that the genes you inherit and not just shared environmental factors (such as diet or social status) are involved in determining your blood pressure.

> Between 20 and 40% of the variation in blood pressure between individuals is a consequence of inherited (genetic) factors.

Salt and high blood pressure

Years of scientific evidence point to the fact that we have too much salt in our diets. By limiting our intake of salt, we can bring about significant reductions in our blood pressure. Current advice suggests that you should

reduce your total salt intake to less than
6 grams per day (that's about 1 teaspoon).

Most processed foods, including breads
and cereals, ready meals and sauces, contain
large quantities of salt. This is why it's
important to be aware of how much hidden
salt you are consuming. It's also another good
reason to stick to freshly prepared foods
wherever possible.

Remember, a lot of the salt we eat is hidden!

Alcohol and high blood pressure

Drinking too much alcohol can increase your
blood pressure and increases your risk of
cardiovascular complications. Current UK
guidelines suggest that men with high blood
pressure should drink no more than 21 units of
alcohol per week (that's about 10 pints of
average strength beer or lager per week),
whilst women should limit their drinking to less
than 14 units per week.

Binge drinking is a known risk factor for stroke.

Bodyweight and high blood pressure

As a population we are becoming increasingly overweight. This is unhealthy for a number of reasons. When it comes to blood pressure, in general the heavier you get, the higher your blood pressure climbs.

Your body mass is measured as a body mass index (BMI), which is a measure of both your height and your weight. Obesity is defined as a BMI of greater than 30 kg/m^2 (kilograms per metre squared). You can easily calculate your own BMI, using the box opposite.

MEASURING YOUR WAIST CIRCUMFERENCE

- The circumference (or distance around) your waist can provide a good indication of the amount of excess fat you have on your abdomen. Waist circumference is closely tied in with cardiovascular risk.
- Measure your waist circumference at the midpoint between the lower border of your ribs and the upper border of your pelvis.
- For men, a waist circumference greater than 102 cm (or 88 cm for women) indicates an increased health risk.

CALCULATE YOUR OWN BODY MASS INDEX (BMI)

It's very simple to work out your own BMI, to see whether your weight has put you at risk of high blood pressure. Grab a tape measure, a set of bathroom scales and a calculator and follow these two steps.

- Measure your height in metres. Multiply this number by itself and write down the answer.
- Measure your weight in kilograms. Divide it by the number you wrote down in the first step. *The number you get is your BMI.*

For example: if your height is 1.80 metres, when you multiply this by itself you get 3.24. If your weight is 80 kilograms, divide 80 by 3.24 to give 24.7.

	18.5	25	30	40
Underweight	Ideal weight	Overweight	Obese	Very obese

Remember though that your BMI is only a broad indicator – it is affected by your body style – people with a very muscular build will have a higher BMI but may not be unhealthily fat. Your age and gender also affect your BMI. Some experts say that men can have a slightly higher BMI before they are at risk, probably due to the fact that they are usually more muscular than women. However, it is best to stick to the guidelines above – they are the internationally accepted boundaries for both genders. The BMI scale does not apply to children though, or during pregnancy.

Calculate your BMI at www.bestmedicine.com

Diet and high blood pressure

Diet is a vital factor in determining your blood pressure. The majority of people in the UK do not eat enough fresh fruit and vegetables. Yet increasing your intake can actually reduce your blood pressure.

Adopting a diet that is low in saturated fat, cholesterol and total fat, and high in fruits and vegetables and low-fat dairy products has been clinically proven to reduce blood pressure. This diet should also include whole grain products, fish, poultry and nuts, and reduced amounts of red meat, sweets and sugar-containing drinks.

Exercise and high blood pressure

In the UK, rates of physical activity are low. Up to three-quarters of all adults do less than the recommended level of exercise each week.

People who lead inactive lifestyles are much more likely to have high blood pressure. Participating in regular exercise not only helps us to stay in shape and maintain a normal bodyweight but can also actively lower blood pressure. If you have high blood pressure, moderate aerobic exercise for 30 minutes at a time for several days each week can reduce blood pressure. Types of exercise that are appropriate to control blood pressure include:

- walking
- cycling
- swimming
- aerobics.

AIM TO EAT

- At least five portions of fresh fruit and vegetables every day.
- Low-fat dairy produce regularly.
- More unsaturated fats (i.e. polyunsaturated and monounsaturated fats).

TRY TO AVOID

- Being overweight.
- Processed foods which contain too much fat, sugar and salt.
- Fatty foods, especially saturated fats and trans fats.
- Salt at the table and in cooking.

Diabetes, the metabolic syndrome and high blood pressure

If you have diabetes then you are twice as likely to have high blood pressure. The reasons for the close association between diabetes and high blood pressure are not entirely clear, but the two conditions appear to share similar risk factors. Shared lifestyle factors may be responsible for the association between the two conditions. For example, consumption of an excessive amount of fat in the diet, which is common amongst people with type 2 diabetes, may affect blood vessels, making them stiffer. This can lead to increases in blood pressure and cause high blood pressure. If you would like to know more, please see *A Simple Guide to Type 2 Diabetes*.

The metabolic syndrome is a collection of factors which increases the likelihood of heart disease, stroke and diabetes. High blood pressure is one of its defining features. Other elements of the metabolic syndrome include abdominal obesity, dyslipidaemia (a disruption in the balance of fats in the blood) and high levels of glucose in the blood. By managing the different components of the syndrome, including high blood pressure, you will also be lowering your risk of other cardiovascular complications.

WHAT ARE THE CONSEQUENCES OF HIGH BLOOD PRESSURE?

If you have been diagnosed with high blood pressure and are following the management plan that you and your doctor have agreed upon, then your chances of suffering any serious long-term consequences are reduced. However, if it is left uncontrolled, high blood pressure can lead to some serious complications.

Heart failure

662,000 people in the UK have definite heart failure, and the condition is on the increase.

The term 'heart failure' is often confused with 'heart attack', but these are in fact quite different things. Heart failure is the term used to describe a condition where the heart becomes progressively less efficient at its job of pumping blood around our bodies. As it becomes progressively less able to cope, it causes back pressure in the system which results in fluid leaking from the smallest capillaries in our lungs, causing breathlessness, and in our feet and ankles, causing swelling.

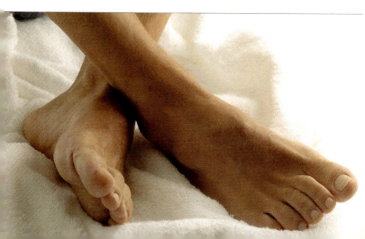

Angina

Angina is a very uncomfortable feeling or pain in the chest. This alarming chest pain can spread to the arms, neck, jaw, back or stomach. It arises because the heart muscle does not get enough oxygen. Angina is usually triggered by exertion or exercise and fades on resting within 10 to 15 minutes.

As we get older, and particularly if we have not been eating and living healthily and exercising regularly, an accumulation of fat in our artery walls makes them narrow and stiff. High blood pressure is one of the major factors in causing blood vessels to stiffen. It is also responsible for the changes in blood flow in the arteries, making the flow more turbulent. If blood flow to our heart becomes disrupted during times when we need more oxygen than normal, there is just not enough oxygen available and our heart is put under excessive strain. Drug treatment aimed at opening up (dilating) the coronary arteries to improve blood flow can help and one of these drugs (called a nitrate) can be sprayed under the tongue and works almost immediately.

If your symptoms of angina are severe then your doctor may need to refer you to hospital for treatment. You may need to have either coronary angioplasty or coronary bypass surgery.

> Over 28,000 patients have coronary bypass surgery in the UK each year.

Heart attack

A heart attack is known medically as a myocardial infarction (or MI) because it happens when parts of the 'myocardium' or heart muscle, 'infarcts' or dies. The underlying cause of a heart attack is identical to the cause of angina, and therefore high blood pressure plays a pivotal role in this too. A heart attack is usually triggered by a blood clot forming in the artery. Taking a 75mg aspirin tablet every day can help patients at risk of a heart attack as aspirin reduces the stickiness of our blood and can even help to dissolve some blood clots if taken during a heart attack.

High blood pressure and stroke

High blood pressure can be an underlying cause of the two most common types – ischaemic and haemorrhagic strokes.

The most common type of stroke (about 80% of all cases) is called an ischaemic stroke. This occurs because the flow of blood through the arteries of the brain is disrupted in a similar way to how blood flow is disrupted in the coronary arteries during a heart attack or in angina. This deprives the brain of oxygen and nutrients. Haemorrhagic strokes (about 20% of all cases) occur when a blood vessel in or near the brain bursts, primarily because of persistent high blood pressure. This causes blood to seep into the spaces between brain cells. Whilst they are not as common as ischaemic strokes, their complications can be more serious.

why me?

Symptoms of stroke can include:
- numbness, weakness or paralysis on one side of the body
- slurred speech or difficulty finding words or understanding speech
- sudden loss of vision or part of a field of vision, dizziness, confusion, unsteadiness or severe headache.

Around 130,000 people in the UK have a stroke every year. That's about one person every 5 minutes.

HIGH BLOOD PRESSURE AND KIDNEY DISEASE

The kidneys are responsible for filtering waste products from the blood and balancing fluid and salt levels in the body.

Kidney failure occurs when the kidneys become less able to remove toxic waste and excess water, and the condition tends to worsen over a period of years. Chronic kidney failure usually leads to so-called end stage renal failure which is fatal unless it is treated either by dialysis (where a machine filters the blood in place of the damaged kidney) or by a kidney transplant. Your kidneys are intrinsically involved in blood pressure regulation and this is why high blood pressure can lead to kidney disease and vice versa.

Over 1.5 million people in the UK have some form of kidney disease.

HIGH BLOOD PRESSURE AND OTHER CIRCULATORY PROBLEMS

- **Legs:** Peripheral arterial disease is the medical name given to disease of the arteries supplying blood to your legs. The causes are the same as those discussed for heart disease, stroke and kidney disease – that is that the arteries are put under excessive stress from the increased blood pressure, and the narrowing of the arteries reduces blood flow. Peripheral arterial disease causes pain in the legs and feet which can make walking difficult.

- **Eyes:** High blood pressure can also lead to narrowed and blocked arteries in the eye, which can cause damage to the retina (the light-sensitive area of the eye). This is called retinal vascular disease. This disease can lead to vision loss and can be an early indicator of heart disease, which is why your doctor will want to take a look at the back of your eye with an instrument called an opthalmoscope.

> Men are six-times more likely to get peripheral arterial disease than women.

BLOOD PRESSURE THROUGH HISTORY

- As long ago as 2,000 B.C. the Chinese "Yellow Emperor" Huang Ti associated salt with a "hardened pulse".
- The structure of the heart was first described in 1706, by Raymond de Viessens, a French anatomy professor.
- The Reverend Stephen Hales first directly measured arterial blood pressure (in a horse!) in the 1700s.
- The mercury column was first used to measure blood pressure in the 1800s.
- The electrocardiogram (ECG) was invented in 1902 by the Dutch physiologist Willem Einthoven. This test is still used today to measure the rate and rhythm of the heart.
- The first drugs to effectively lower blood pressure were introduced in the 1950s.
- In 1971, Kannel, Gordon and Schwartz showed that systolic blood pressure was a better predictor of heart disease than diastolic blood pressure – until this time systolic blood pressure was largely ignored and deemed a natural consequence of ageing.

ARTERIAL BLOOD PRESSURE WAS FIRST MEASURED IN A HORSE.

simple science

SIMPLE SCIENCE

The control of blood pressure within the body is very complex. Blood pressure is managed by your heart, your nervous system, the blood vessels of your circulatory system and the kidneys, and is influenced by many different factors.

In order to understand how our blood pressure is controlled by the body under normal circumstances and to appreciate how the drugs that are used to lower blood pressure actually work, we first need to understand a little bit of the science involved in these processes.

HOW DOES THE BODY CONTROL BLOOD PRESSURE?

Blood pressure is closely controlled by several physiological processes that act together in concert. It is these mechanisms which ensure enough blood flows through our circulation and allows our tissues to be supplied with appropriate nutrients for them to function properly. When any of these mechanisms are disrupted, high blood pressure can result.

Blood pressure is regulated by a series of nerves and hormones that monitor the volume of blood in the circulation, the diameter of the blood vessels and the force of the heartbeat. Each of these factors is intrinsically tied up with how blood pressure is regulated in our blood vessels.

Blood pressure depends on the strength of the heartbeat, the diameter of the blood vessels and the volume of blood running through the circulation. It's a bit like the water pressure coming from a garden hose. You can increase the strength of the water flow either by turning on the tap a bit more (equivalent to the heart beating more powerfully and faster) or by tightening the nozzle and increasing the resistance to water flowing out of the hose (equivalent to the vessels narrowing or constricting).

The complexity of blood pressure control helps to explain why there are so many different drugs available to treat high blood pressure. Each of the five main classes of blood pressure-lowering drugs has different effects and targets these different blood pressure-controlling mechanisms.

BASICS OF BLOOD PRESSURE CONTROL

To summarise, there are a number of mechanisms by which the body can alter blood pressure.

- By altering the strength and frequency by which the heart pumps blood around the circulation.
- By altering the diameter of the blood vessels.
- By altering the volume of blood in the circulation.

These main processes are controlled automatically in our bodies and balance is maintained by our **autonomic nervous system** and our **kidneys**.

CONTROL OF BLOOD PRESSURE BY THE AUTONOMIC NERVOUS SYSTEM

'Autonomic' refers to the part of our nervous system that regulates essential functions without us having to think about it (like our heart rate and how we breathe). The autonomic nervous system has two main divisions – the **sympathetic** and **parasympathetic** nervous systems, which work in opposite directions to ensure that essential functions are kept in balance. The autonomic nervous system plays a major role in controlling our blood pressure.

- The sympathetic nervous system accelerates the heart rate, constricts blood vessels and raises blood pressure.

simple science

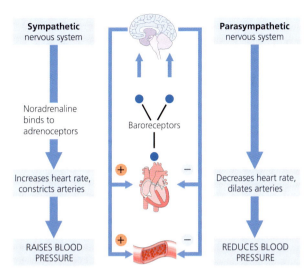

THE ROLE OF THE NERVOUS SYSTEM IN THE CONTROL OF BLOOD PRESSURE.

- The parasympathetic nervous system slows the heart rate, dilates blood vessels and reduces blood pressure.

Within certain blood vessels, there are a collection of receptors which actively sense changes in our blood pressure. These structures are called 'baroreceptors' ('baro' meaning pressure, just think of a **baro**meter). The baroreceptors essentially monitor the amount of stretch in the major blood vessels, which reflects the amount of pressure in the circulation. If the pressure is too high or too low, the baroreceptors send messages to the heart and other blood vessels via the nerve fibres of the sympathetic nervous system, in order to correct it.

All nerves need neurotransmitters (chemical messengers) to work. In the case of the sympathetic nervous system, the main chemical messengers are the hormones, **noradrenaline** and **adrenaline**. Noradrenaline is important in blood pressure control for two main reasons.

1. It binds to specific receptors found in heart muscle (beta-adrenoreceptors). The heart responds by increasing the strength and frequency of the heartbeat that in turn results in an increase in blood pressure.

2. It binds to specific receptors within the muscle that lines blood vessels (mainly alpha-adrenoreceptors). This causes the muscle of the blood vessels to constrict, which in turn reduces blood flow through the vessel and thereby increases blood pressure.

The main effect of the **beta-blocker** class of blood pressure-lowering drugs is to block the binding of noradrenaline to the beta-adrenoreceptors of the heart, thereby slowing and reducing the strength of the heartbeat.

The **alpha-blocker** class of blood pressure-lowering drugs (which are used much less frequently to treat high blood pressure these days) work mainly by blocking the binding of noradrenaline to the alpha-adrenoreceptors in the muscle that lines the blood vessels. This causes the vessels to dilate giving more room for the blood to occupy and so reducing blood pressure.

simple science

THE KIDNEYS AND BLOOD PRESSURE CONTROL

The sympathetic nervous system also stimulates the kidneys to retain salt and water, and thereby increases the volume of blood and thus blood pressure.

The kidneys are two bean-shaped organs, each about the size of a human fist, which are located on the right and left side of the body at the back of the abdomen. The kidneys perform many vital functions. Whilst most people correctly think of the kidneys as a type of waste-removal system, the kidneys are also essential for maintaining the balance of fluids in the body by controlling the amount of salt and therefore water we excrete in our urine. It is this last function which is intrinsically tied up with the control of blood pressure. In general, the more fluid in the circulation, the higher the blood pressure, and therefore, by altering blood volume, blood pressure is changed.

The total amount of blood in our circulation passes through our kidneys about 60 times per day.

The **diuretic** class of blood pressure-lowering drugs work by making our kidneys remove more salt from our bloodstream which attracts water with it. We urinate more as a result, the volume of blood in our circulation decreases and our blood pressure falls.

If we have too much salt in our bodies (for example as a result of having too much salt in our diet) then our body attempts to reduce the concentration of this excess salt by diluting it with water via something called osmosis. This process ensures that the concentration of salt is balanced inside and outside a cell. We get thirsty and drink more to compensate but instead of excreting this we absorb it into our bloodstream. The volume of blood in circulation increases and so does our blood pressure.

> Osmosis describes how water follows salt concentrations across a membrane, like the ones which cover every cell of our bodies.

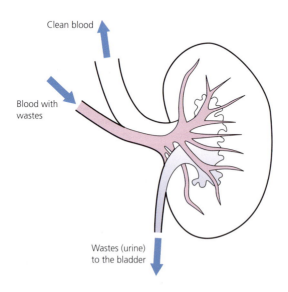

To summarise the process, the following steps occur in the kidney to maintain blood pressure control.

1. The kidneys respond directly to changes in blood pressure.

2. If blood pressure increases, the kidneys are stimulated to increase their excretion of salt and water in the urine, leading to a reduction in blood volume and return of blood pressure to normal.

3. If blood pressure decreases, the kidneys decrease their excretion of salt and water, so that blood volume increases and blood pressure returns to normal.

The structure in the kidney which regulates the uptake or excretion of salt is known as a 'nephron'. Each kidney contains about a million nephrons. You can probably visualise how small and how delicate the nephrons are. Each nephron has many tubes and loops where salts and other components are filtered from the blood and then discarded in our urine. Drugs such as the diuretics act within the nephron and encourage excessive salt and thus fluid to be eliminated in the urine, thereby lowering blood volume and blood pressure.

The blood pressure-altering effects of the renin–angiotensin system (see the following section) are also exerted at the kidney.

HORMONAL CONTROL OF BLOOD PRESSURE: THE RENIN–ANGIOTENSIN SYSTEM

Our kidneys also control blood pressure through the activity of the renin–angiotensin system. This system involves a chain of complex chemical events, which act together to control our blood pressure by altering the balance of sodium in our bodies.

To simplify the processes which occur in the renin–angiotensin system, it is best to consider the key events as a series of steps.

1. The liver releases a protein called angiotensinogen into our circulation.
2. As part of the complex balancing act of blood pressure control performed automatically by our bodies, and in response to falls in blood pressure, our kidneys release renin.
3. Renin, an enzyme, acts on angiotensinogen and converts it into a different protein called angiotensin I. Both of these proteins are essentially inactive and do not have any direct effect on blood pressure control until they are activated by yet another enzyme.
4. This enzyme is called angiotensin-converting enzyme (shortened to ACE) and is released by the cells which line our blood vessels. These cells are called endothelial cells.
5. ACE works by converting the inactive angiotensin I into the active angiotensin II.

An enzyme is a biological catalyst.

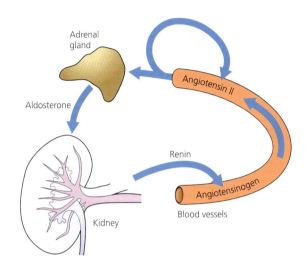

THE RENIN–ANGIOTENSIN SYSTEM.

Angiotensin II actively raises blood pressure through two main effects.

1. Angiotensin II acts directly on the walls of blood vessels making them contract and causing them to narrow. In doing this, blood cannot flow so freely and therefore blood pressure increases. Because of this function, angiotensin II is also called a **vasoconstrictor**.
2. Angiotensin II stimulates our adrenal glands (two small glands that are perched up on the top of our kidneys) to release another hormone called aldosterone. Aldosterone causes sodium to be reclaimed by the kidney, which in turn attracts water via osmosis leading to an increase in blood pressure.

Given the pivotal role of the renin–angiotensin system in controlling blood pressure, many of the drugs that have been developed to lower blood pressure have been specifically designed to interfere with these processes. These drugs fall into two classes.

1. The **ACE inhibitors**, which work directly by stopping the angiotensin-converting enzyme (ACE) from turning inactive angiotensin I into active angiotensin II.
2. The **angiotensin receptor blockers**, which work by stopping the active angiotensin II from reaching the receptors that trigger its blood pressure-lowering effects.

THE ROLE OF CALCIUM IN BLOOD PRESSURE CONTROL

Calcium is vital for the contraction and relaxation of all types of muscle in our bodies. An increase in calcium within cells is a trigger which causes the contraction (tensing) of all muscle types.

Calcium enters muscle cells through calcium channels, which are proteins embedded in the cell wall which recognise calcium and allow it to enter. The orchestrated contraction of muscle cells is what makes the whole muscle contract and perform work.

In the circulation calcium is one trigger that makes the muscles that line your arteries constrict and narrow, thereby causing an increase in blood pressure. Any agent which blocks the entry of calcium would therefore be expected to reduce blood pressure.

This is one way that the **calcium-channel blocker** class of blood pressure-lowering drugs works.

Given that the heart is a muscular organ, calcium is also needed for the generation and control of our heartbeats. The force of our heartbeats is influenced by the amount of calcium in our blood. Therefore, drugs which block, inhibit or antagonise (these words essentially mean the same thing) calcium channels can influence the force of the heartbeat too and consequently, our blood pressure. Thus, calcium-channel blockers reduce blood pressure by both preventing the influx of calcium in the muscles that line our arteries and in the heart muscle itself.

SUMMARY

- Blood pressure is regulated by many different processes in the body, and is under the control of both the nervous system and the kidneys.
- The salt in our diets affects blood pressure because it is linked to blood volume.
- Both blood volume and salt concentrations are regulated by the kidneys, and drugs such as the diuretics control blood pressure by their effects on fluid control.
- Renin is released from the kidney in response to low blood pressure and is converted into angiotensin II and stimulates the production of aldosterone – two important controllers of blood pressure.
- Different classes of antihypertensive drugs lower blood pressure by targeting these systems directly. Some blood pressure-lowering drugs act by affecting calcium concentrations in the cell or by blocking the effects of adrenaline via alpha- or beta-adrenoceptors.

managing high blood pressure

MANAGING HIGH BLOOD PRESSURE

If you have recently been diagnosed with high blood pressure then it is only natural that you will worry how it will affect your daily life. Millions of people with hypertension continue to lead normal lives. There's no reason why you can't take control of the condition and continue to lead a full and active life.

THE GOOD NEWS

It may sound strange, but in some respects you are quite lucky if your high blood pressure has been diagnosed. You will now be well on your way to receiving the appropriate care that you will need to ensure that your blood pressure is adequately controlled and your risk of more serious cardiovascular complications is significantly reduced. Many people in the UK are unlucky in that they are walking around with high blood pressure that has not yet been detected, and consequently their health remains at risk from this 'silent killer'.

This section will explain in more detail how your doctor diagnoses high blood pressure and will describe some of the recommendations that he or she is likely to make for reducing it. This may be advice to change some aspects of your lifestyle, such as doing more exercise and adopting a healthier diet, both of which have been proven to significantly reduce blood pressure, as well as improving your general well-being. Alternatively, you may be given medication to help you lower your blood pressure.

AVOID DRINKING COFFEE IMMEDIATELY BEFORE YOU HAVE YOUR BLOOD PRESSURE MEASURED.

DIAGNOSIS

In order to diagnose high blood pressure, your doctor will need to measure your blood pressure. He or she will normally do this during a routine appointment. Your doctor may measure your blood pressure with a traditional mercury sphygmomanometer or may use a modern electronic device.

There are a number of steps you can take to ensure that your blood pressure reading is as accurate as it can be.

- Avoid vigorous exercise, tea, coffee or cigarettes for around half an hour before your appointment.
- Be as relaxed as possible. Sit down for at least 5 minutes before your blood pressure is measured.

If your doctor suspects that you have high blood pressure they will measure your blood pressure at least twice before making a firm diagnosis.

All adults should have their blood pressure measured at least once every 5 years.

DIAGNOSIS IN DIABETIC OR ELDERLY PATIENTS

If you have diabetes or are elderly your doctor may wish to take an additional blood pressure reading with you in a standing position. This is because you may be at increased risk of a condition known as 'orthostatic hypotension'. If you are diagnosed with orthostatic hypotension then you may be referred to a specialist.

WHAT IS ORTHOSTATIC HYPOTENSION?

This is a sudden drop in systolic blood pressure of at least 20 mmHg (or a drop in diastolic blood pressure of at least 10 mmHg) within 3 minutes of standing up. It may be accompanied by symptoms such as dizziness and fainting. It often affects people with diabetes or elderly people, and is also sometimes a side-effect of drugs.

managing high blood pressure

MEASURING BLOOD PRESSURE WITH A TRADITIONAL MERCURY SPHYGMOMANOMETER

- Your arm should be supported at the level of your heart with no tight clothing squeezing your arm.
- The doctor or nurse will place a cuff of an appropriate size around your upper arm with the rubber tube leading away from your inner elbow over your brachial artery (the artery that runs from the shoulder to the elbow).
- The doctor or nurse will ensure that the mercury column is vertical and at eye level.
- The cuff may be inflated briefly in order to estimate the systolic pressure.
- The cuff will be inflated to 30 mmHg above the estimated systolic pressure – this will feel a little uncomfortable but it won't last too long.
- A stethoscope will be placed at your inner elbow and the cuff slowly deflated.
- As the cuff is deflated your blood flow returns, turbulently at first, and this makes the sounds which your doctor can hear with his stethoscope.
- The first sounds your doctor or nurse hears are characteristic of systolic blood pressure – the doctor or nurse will read the pressure from the mercury column at this point.
- The diastolic blood pressure is read from the mercury column when these sounds disappear.

24-HOUR AMBULATORY BLOOD PRESSURE MONITORING

Ambulatory literally means that you are free to walk around.

In certain instances (for example, if you are pregnant) your doctor may wish to gather a more detailed impression of your blood pressure and how it changes over an entire 24-hour period. To do this you may be given a 24-hour ambulatory blood pressure monitor. This device records your blood pressure for the entire 24-hour period and stores the information for your doctor to examine at a later time. Your doctor may wish to perform this type of monitoring if your blood pressure is only just bordering on being high, if you suffer from fainting spells, are pregnant, or if your doctor suspects you may have 'white coat hypertension'. Some people find these rather inconvenient and more commonly you may be loaned an electronic device and given clear instructions about how and when to record your own blood pressure at home.

HOME MONITORING

Electronic blood pressure monitors are increasingly being used in doctors' surgeries in place of the traditional mercury column sphygmomanometer. These devices are also being used by people in their own homes. If you decide you would like to monitor your blood pressure at home then it is important to purchase a reliable machine. The British Hypertension Society has produced a list of devices to help you choose which one to buy (*www.bhsoc.org*). These devices are available in most high street pharmacies and your pharmacist will also be happy to offer advice on choosing one that meets your needs.

Some machines measure blood pressure from the wrist or finger. However, these are generally less reliable and so it is recommended that you use a machine which measures blood pressure at the upper arm (the cuff is designed to fit the arm above your elbow). This will also give you a reading which is similar to that which your doctor measures. You may also find that the monitor you choose has a range of cuff sizes available. The better the cuff size fits your arm, the more accurate the blood pressure reading will be.

Your blood pressure reading will generally be a little lower when measured at home than when it is measured at your doctor's surgery or in hospital.

White coat hypertension refers to blood pressure which is only high when measured at the doctor's surgery, clinic or hospital. It is a subconscious stressful reaction to the medical environment (hence the term 'white coat'). White coat hypertension does not generally require treatment.

HOW HIGH IS HIGH?

Bodies such as the World Health Organization and the British Hypertension Society have an interest in the problem of high blood pressure and the impact that it has on our nation's health.

The severity of high blood pressure varies significantly from one person to the next. The table below shows the different categories of hypertension that have been agreed upon by several committees (such as the World Health Organization and the British Hypertension Society). By defining different levels of severity, our doctors will be able to make tailored decisions on when and how to treat high blood pressure.

COULD MY HIGH BLOOD PRESSURE BE A SIGN OF SOMETHING ELSE?

The majority of cases of hypertension are known as essential hypertension. This means that the cause of high blood pressure is unclear. It is very likely that the condition has

THE DIFFERENT SEVERITIES OF HIGH BLOOD PRESSURE

Category	Systolic blood pressure (mmHg)	Diastolic blood pressure (mmHg)
Blood pressure		
Optimal	Below 120	Below 80
Normal	Below 130	Below 85
High normal	130–139	85–89
Hypertension		
Mild (grade 1)	140–159	90–99
Moderate (grade 2)	160–179	100–109
Severe (grade 3)	180 and higher	110 and higher
Isolated systolic hypertension[a]		
Grade 1	140–159	Under 90
Grade 2	160 and higher	Under 90

[a] Isolated systolic hypertension means that your diastolic blood pressure is normal but your systolic blood pressure is too high. This situation is very common in the elderly.

CAUSES OF SECONDARY HYPERTENSION

	Description
Reaction to drugs	Examples include ibuprofen, oral contraceptives and corticosteroids.
Kidney disease	Existing, previous or family history.
Phaeochromocytoma	Over production of the hormones, adrenaline or noradrenaline, from the adrenal gland (small glands that sit on top of the kidneys).
Conn's syndrome (also called primary aldosteronism or hyperaldosteronism)	Over production of aldosterone from the adrenal glands. High levels of aldosterone cause sodium retention and consequently high blood pressure.
Coarctation	Narrowing of a blood vessel, commonly the aorta, present from birth.
Cushing's syndrome	Raised levels of glucocorticoid hormones produced by the adrenal gland.
Hypo- or hyperthyroidism	Deficiency or over activity of the thyroid gland.

arisen as a result of a number of different problems, with lifestyle factors playing a pivotal role. This includes problems like being overweight, not taking enough exercise and drinking too much alcohol.

In contrast, about 5% of patients will be diagnosed with secondary hypertension, which refers to a type of high blood pressure with a known cause. This can include a reaction to the combined oral contraceptive pill or another medication you may be taking. It may also be a symptom of an underlying disease such as kidney disease or one of the conditions described in the table above. In general, individuals with secondary hypertension develop high blood pressure at a younger age and their blood pressure can be much harder to control.

WHAT OTHER TESTS IS MY DOCTOR LIKELY TO CONDUCT?

As high blood pressure is a major risk factor for heart disease, strokes and disorders of the kidney and eyes, your doctor is likely to run the following tests to rule out these conditions:

- blood test
- urine test
- physical examination
- electrocardiogram (ECG).

For example, you may have a blood sample taken so that your blood fats can be measured. Like high blood pressure, high levels of the blood fats – cholesterol and triglycerides – are risk factors for heart disease, stroke, metabolic syndrome or diabetes. Your blood glucose level – an indicator of diabetes – may also be

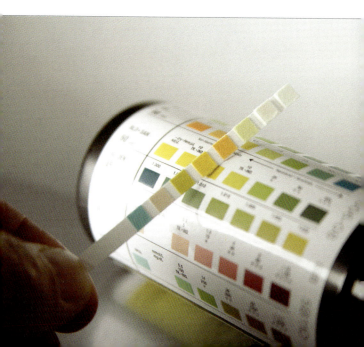

WHAT IS AN ECG?

ECG stands for electrocardiogram and is a test for measuring the rhythm and rate of your heart. It plays an important role in the diagnosis of cardiovascular disease. You will be asked to lie down and electrodes will be attached to various parts of your body – these are just to measure the electrical activity of your heart from different angles. A person who has had high blood pressure for a long period may have an enlarged heart (due to the extra work it has to perform to pump blood around the body) and this may be detected on an ECG. The whole test should only take a few minutes.

checked, and you may be asked to provide a urine sample so that your kidney function can be checked. Your doctor may conduct a physical examination to check your eyes, your heart and your pulses. He or she may also request that you have a chest X-ray or an ECG.

Your doctor will ask you questions about your lifestyle, your diet, how active you are, your smoking and drinking habits and whether or not you have any family history of specific illnesses. It is important to tell your doctor if you are taking any over-the-counter medicines such as aspirin or other anti-inflammatory drugs, and you should also tell them if you are taking any complementary medicines like herbs or supplements.

BLOOD PRESSURE MANAGEMENT PROGRAMME

If your doctor or nurse discovers that you have high blood pressure, your doctor will discuss with you a blood pressure management programme. It is very important that you play an active role in discussing and directing your programme in partnership with your doctor or nurse. This will ensure that you have the best chance of controlling your blood pressure.

The advice your doctor gives you regarding managing your blood pressure will vary according to:

- how high your blood pressure is
- how long your blood pressure has been high
- whether or not you have any other medical conditions (e.g. diabetes or kidney problems)
- whether or not you have any other risk factors for cardiovascular disease.

If your blood pressure is extremely high (above 180/110 mmHg) then you will almost certainly be prescribed antihypertensive drugs immediately. If you have diabetes or you have been diagnosed with cardiovascular disease or kidney disease then good control of your blood pressure is even more important and drug treatment is also likely to be initiated immediately. If you have less severe hypertension then your doctor will usually give you advice on how to alter your lifestyle to lower your blood pressure. Many of these lifestyle changes are common sense and include changes to your diet, increasing your physical activity and losing excessive weight. You may even be prescribed a course at the local gym. After these changes to your lifestyle have had the chance to take effect, you will be given an appointment to return and have your blood pressure checked again. Your return appointment could be within a couple of weeks, a few months, or you may even be asked to make another appointment in a year if your blood pressure is only slightly raised. At this point your doctor will assess whether the changes you have made to your lifestyle have been sufficient to lower your blood pressure. If they are not, then you may be started on a course of drug treatment.

LIFESTYLE CHANGES

The lifestyle changes that your doctor recommends for you are also good for everyone to follow, whether or not they have high blood pressure. If you and your family adopt a healthy lifestyle sooner rather than later, then the chances that all of you will develop high blood pressure are greatly reduced.

Some of the recommended lifestyle changes that will reduce your blood pressure and lower your risk of cardiovascular disease include:

- maintaining a normal bodyweight
- reducing your daily salt intake
- limiting your alcohol consumption
- reducing your consumption of saturated and total fat, and cholesterol
- increasing the amount of fresh fruit and vegetables in your diet
- doing at least 30 minutes of exercise each day on most days of the week
- giving up smoking.

Reducing salt intake

The chemical name for salt is sodium chloride; it is the sodium in salt which raises blood pressure.

Too much salt can cause our blood pressure to rise to harmful levels. Current guidelines from the British Hypertension Society recommend that our daily sodium intake should be limited to less than 2.4 g each day. This is equivalent to about 6 g of salt, which is about 1 teaspoon per day.

Five ways to reduce your salt intake.
- Do not add salt to your food at the table.
- Do not add salt to your food when you cook.
- Use herbs and spices to flavour your food rather than using salt.
- Learn how much salt is in sauces, dressings and processed foods, and cut back on their use.
- Avoid high sodium foods like crisps, salted peanuts, processed meats and cheeses.

It is also important to remember that there is a lot of hidden sodium in our foods, particularly in foods that are highly processed. This includes things like baking additives (sodium bicarbonate), flavour enhancers (monosodium glutamate), sweeteners (sodium saccharin), preservatives (sodium nitrite) and antioxidants (sodium ascorbate).

Reducing excessive bodyweight

In the UK, over 1 in 5 boys and 1 in 4 girls are now either overweight or obese.

In general, the heavier you are, the higher your blood pressure will be. If you adopt a healthy lifestyle with regular exercise and a balanced diet then you should be able to lose weight and lower your blood pressure in a controlled manner. Luckily, many of the measures that you adopt to help you lose weight will, in themselves, help to lower your blood pressure. Losing weight may also reduce your risk of developing diabetes, cardiovascular disease and cancer. There are some useful links at the back of this book to help you find the best way to lose weight sensibly and to maintain your normal bodyweight over the longer term.

Limit excessive alcohol consumption

Moderate consumption of alcohol as part of a healthy and varied diet is not harmful to your health. However, drinking excessive amounts of alcohol has been linked to harmful increases in blood pressure. Binge drinking is thought to be particularly dangerous to your health since it has been associated with stroke. Women should aim to consume no more than 14 units of alcohol per week whilst men should not exceed 21 units per week.

Type of alcoholic drink (ABV [alcohol by volume])	How much?	How many units?
Average strength beer/lager	Half pint	1
Spirit	One pub measure (25 mL)	1
Wine (11–12% ABV)	Small glass (125 mL)	1.5
Beer/lager/cider – bottled	One bottle (330 mL)	1.5
'Alcopop' (4–6% ABV)	One bottle (330 mL)	1.3–2

Exercise

Aerobic exercise encourages the circulation of oxygen through the blood and includes cycling, swimming, running and brisk walking.

For many of us, devising a regular exercise plan to fit around our hectic schedules can be a real challenge. Exercise should be regular and aerobic for it to be of benefit when it comes to lowering blood pressure.

We are advised to exercise for at least 30 minutes at a time, on most days of the week. For a lot of busy people, particularly those with families or demanding work schedules, it can be especially hard to work out where to fit this exercise in. It is worthwhile taking time to plan exactly how you intend to introduce exercise into your life. You will soon reap the benefits both in terms of self-satisfaction and your general well-being. However, make sure you talk to your doctor before you embark on any new exercise plan, particularly if you have another illness such as back pain, arthritis or osteoporosis.

Be realistic about your exercise goals.

LIFESTYLE MEASURES AND BLOOD PRESSURE REDUCTION

Intervention	Recommendation
Weight reduction	Stay slim – achieve a body mass index (BMI) of 20–25 kg/m^2.
Reduce sodium intake	Eat less salt – your daily sodium intake should be under 2.4 g (equivalent to 6 g of salt).
Limit alcohol consumption	Drink less than 21 units per week (men) and 14 units per week (women).
Healthy eating	Eat more fruit, vegetables and low-fat dairy products. Eat less saturated fat.
Physical activity	Take regular aerobic exercise – at least 30 minutes a day and at least three times a week.

managing high blood pressure

EIGHT WAYS TO INCREASE EXERCISE

1. Allow time to walk the kids to school.
2. Fit in a half hour swim at the local pool before setting off for work in the morning.
3. Cycle to work for 2 or 3 days of the week.
4. Fit a short run into each day – start gently and build up slowly!
5. Be strict with yourself, leave your desk and take a brisk walk at lunchtime!
6. Go ice-skating, rollerblading, swimming or cycling one evening a week with family or friends.
7. Learn a new activity; join a tennis or badminton club, or learn to dance.
8. Take the stairs not the lift or escalator.

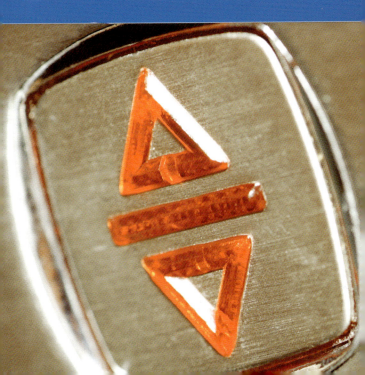

Fat and cholesterol

Too much cholesterol in the blood can lodge in your arteries and ultimately block your circulation.

Monounsaturated fats (e.g. olive oil) and polyunsaturated fats (e.g. the omega-3 fats found in oily fish) have been shown in some studies to reduce cholesterol levels and lower blood pressure, and may be beneficial in reducing your risk for heart disease. It is advisable, therefore, to replace saturated fats with monounsaturated fats and omega-3 polyunsaturated fats to help you lower your blood pressure and reduce your cardiovascular risk.

GOOD FATS... BAD FATS

Good fats:

Omega-3 polyunsaturated fats are found in oily fish, flaxseed oil, walnut oil and fish oil.

Monounsaturated fats are found in olive oil, rapeseed oil, nuts, seeds and avocado.

Bad fats:

Trans fat (or trans fatty acids) are found in highly processed foods (like biscuits or margarine) and increase cholesterol in the blood.

Saturated fats (or saturated fatty acids) are found in butter, cakes, pastries, biscuits, meat products and cream. They also raise the cholesterol in our blood.

FRUIT AND VEGETABLES

There is clear evidence that increasing your consumption of fruit and vegetables can help to lower your blood pressure. The 'five-a-day' rule should be fairly familiar to all of us now, but increasingly it is advised that we eat more than five portions of fruit and vegetables each day.

We need to change the focus of our diets so that fresh produce and a full fruit bowl forms the backbone of our meals, rather than just an afterthought. Fruit salads, ripe tomatoes and lush salads dressed with olive oil, and vibrant vegetable based stews (such as ratatouille) conjure up the diet of the Mediterranean. Indeed, much of the inspiration for what is perceived to be healthy eating is drawn from the so-called Mediterranean diet.

One controversy that you may have heard about is whether or not potatoes contribute towards the 'five-a-day' rule. Potatoes are certainly a vegetable and they do contain vitamin C. However, they mostly consist of starchy carbohydrate. This means that potatoes don't really count towards your daily fruit and vegetable intake, and instead are considered to be equivalent to other carbohydrate-rich foods like rice, pasta and breads.

WHAT IS A PORTION?

- A medium sized apple.
- A large handful of grapes or strawberries.
- A bowl of salad.
- A cupful of peas or the equivalent.

THE DRUG TREATMENT OF HIGH BLOOD PRESSURE

There are several situations where you may be offered antihypertensive drugs almost immediately. These include:

- having a blood pressure greater than 180/110 mmHg
- having a blood pressure greater than 160/100 mmHg that persists over time
- having a blood pressure greater than 140/90 mmHg plus one or more of the following:
  - diabetes
  - 'target organ damage' (e.g. heart or kidney disease, or stroke)
  - a 10-year cardiovascular risk greater than 20%.

However, if your blood pressure is only mildly increased (less than 140/90 mmHg) then you are likely only to require drug therapy for your hypertension if the lifestyle changes your doctor recommends have not brought about a large enough reduction in your blood pressure.

Clinical trials have shown that all of these different classes of drugs are roughly equivalent in their ability to reduce blood

managing high blood pressure

> **There are five major classes of drugs currently used to lower blood pressure:**
>
> - diuretics (e.g. bendroflumethiazide [Aprinox®], chlortalidone [Hygroton®])
> - alpha-blockers (e.g. doxazosin [Cardura®], terazosin [Hytrin®])
> - beta-blockers (e.g. atenolol [Tenormin®], bisoprolol [Emcor®])
> - calcium-channel blockers (e.g. amlodipine [Istin®], felodipine [Plendil])
> - angiotensin-converting enzyme (ACE) inhibitors (e.g. perindopril [Coversyl®], ramipril [Tritace®])
> - angiotensin receptor blockers (ARBs) (e.g. losartan [Cozaar®], irbesartan [Aprovel®]).

pressure, and any single agent can reduce blood pressure by about 7 or 8%. However, as larger reductions than this are usually required to allow people to get their blood pressure to a safe level, more than one drug is often required. The choice of drug or drugs depends very much on the individual concerned. It is vitally important that you remember to take these drugs as directed by your doctor in order for them to work properly.

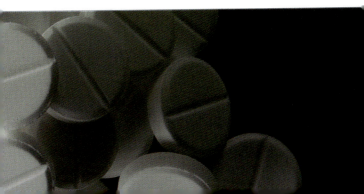

WHICH TYPE OF BLOOD PRESSURE LOWERING DRUG IS BEST?

Lots of clinical trials have been carried out to determine which class of antihypertensive drug is considered to be the best. What these studies have shown is that all of the drugs that we currently use to lower our blood pressure are effective. However, there is some emerging and compelling evidence that there may be some important differences between the different antihypertensive classes and their effects on the complications of high blood pressure. For example, studies have shown that people who take a beta-blocker together with a diuretic may have an increased risk of developing diabetes. In addition, preliminary findings from a large-scale study called ASCOT have shown that significant differences exist between two different types of drug combinations (an ACE inhibitor combined with a calcium-channel blocker compared with a beta-blocker combined with a diuretic). These early findings suggest that there may be real differences between the different groups of drugs which may have a major bearing on how blood pressure is managed in the future. If you are concerned about any aspect of how your high blood pressure is being managed please consult your doctor.

MULTIPLE CAUSES REQUIRE MULTIPLE SOLUTIONS

Given that there are many different causes of hypertension which differ between different people, some types of drugs may be more suited for one person compared with another. Your doctor will take into account your personal history and will use some of the latest guidelines to prescribe you the drug that is most suited to your circumstances. There are around 70 blood pressure-lowering drugs currently available for your doctor to prescribe. So please don't worry if you are on a different drug to other people you know with high blood pressure.

COMMONLY PRESCRIBED ANTIHYPERTENSIVE DRUGS

Drug class and generic name	Brand name
Diuretics	
Bendroflumethiazide	Aprinox®/Neo-NaClex®
Chlortalidone	Hygroton®
Cyclopenthiazide	Navidrex®
Indapamide	Natrilix®
Alpha-blockers	
Doxazosin	Cardura®
Indoramin	Baratol®
Prazosin	Hypovase®
Terazosin	Hytrin®
Beta-blockers	
Atenolol	Tenormin®
Bisoprolol	Cardicor®/Emcor®/Monocor®
Carvedilol	Eucardic®
Propanalol	Inderal®
Metoprolol	Betaloc®
Calcium-channel blockers	
Amlodipine	Istin®/Amlostin®
Diltiazem	Tildiem®
Felodipine	Plendil®/Felotens®/Vascalpha®
Isradipine	Prescal®
Lacidipine	Motens®
Nifedipine	Adalat®
Verapamil	Cordilox®/Securon®
ACE inhibitors	
Captopril	Capoten®
Enalapril	Innovace®
Perindopril	Coversyl®
Ramipril	Tritace®
Angiotensin receptor blockers	
Candesartan	Amias®
Eprosartan	Teveten®
Irbesartan	Aprovel®
Losartan	Cozaar®

Drugs often have more than one name. A generic name, which refers to its active ingredient, and a brand name, which is the trade name given to it by the pharmaceutical company. Captopril is a generic name and Capoten® is a brand name.

COMBINATION ANTIHYPERTENSIVE DRUGS

Combination drug name	Drug 1	Drug 2
Triapin®	Ramipril (ACE inhibitor)	Felodipine (calcium-channel blocker)
Prestim®	Timolol (beta-blocker)	Bendroflumethiazide (thiazide diuretic)
Tenoret®	Atenolol (beta-blocker)	Chlortalidone (thiazide diuretic)
Coaprovel®	Irbesartan (angiotensin receptor blocker)	Hydrochlorothiazide (thiazide diuretic)

COMBINATION DRUGS

The prescription of more than one type of antihypertensive drug to treat high blood pressure is becoming increasingly commonplace. But, since most of us prefer to take as few pills as possible, drug companies are responding by producing combination drugs (i.e. one pill which contains more than one active ingredient).

Often, however, the combination of drugs that your doctor recommends for you is not yet available in a single tablet combination form. In these cases, you will still have to take two or three separate tablets.

THE ABCD RULE

In order to help doctors choose which combinations of antihypertensives to prescribe, the British Hypertension Society has produced a flow chart called the ABCD rule to guide the prescription of the different antihypertensive agents. This may help you to understand why your doctor prescribes you certain drugs.

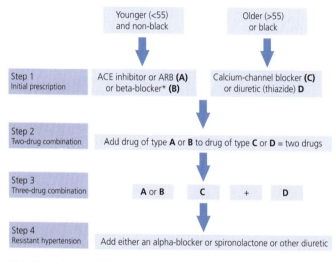

	Younger (<55) and non-black	Older (>55) or black
Step 1 — Initial prescription	ACE inhibitor or ARB **(A)** or beta-blocker* **(B)**	Calcium-channel blocker **(C)** or diuretic (thiazide) **D**
Step 2 — Two-drug combination	Add drug of type **A** or **B** to drug of type **C** or **D** = two drugs	
Step 3 — Three-drug combination	**A** or **B** **C** + **D**	
Step 4 — Resistant hypertension	Add either an alpha-blocker or spironolactone or other diuretic	

*Beta-blockers have recently been associated with increased risk for early-onset diabetes, thus drugs from group A possibly represent first choice.
ARB, angiotensin receptor blocker.

managing high blood pressure

The whole principle underpinning this chart is the likelihood of certain groups of people having high or low levels of a substance called renin, which plays a pivotal role in the renin–angiotensin system (see Simple Science).

- ■ The 'A' (ACE inhibitors and angiotensin receptor blockers) and 'B' (beta-blockers) drugs inhibit this system, thereby resulting in reductions in blood pressure. Therefore, people who have high renin levels should usually use one of these drugs first.
- ■ Older people and those of African or Afro-Caribbean origin are more likely to have lower renin levels. Therefore, in these individuals it is more common to start with drugs that do not work directly on the renin–angiotensin system. Typically these include the 'C' (calcium-channel blockers) and 'D' (diuretics) drugs.
- ■ If blood pressure is not brought under sufficient control with one drug, the next rational step is to use a combination from the two distinct groups (e.g. A + D). If the blood pressure still fails to get to the target level a third drug may be required, and an ideal combination in this case would be A + C + D.

SIDE-EFFECTS OF ANTIHYPERTENSIVE DRUGS

Drugs are taken in order to have a specific effect on a particular pathway, function, organ or phenomenon within the body. However, once taken, drugs will distribute throughout the body and most will cause additional, and unwanted, effects on other parts of the body. These additional effects are known as side-effects and can vary widely from drug to drug. They can either be general unpleasant effects like headaches, stomach aches or dizziness, but can also be abnormalities of chemicals in the blood that will only be detected by your doctor using laboratory tests. If you do experience any kind of side-effect that you think may be linked to your medication then it is important to inform your doctor as soon as possible so that your treatment plan can be looked into and changed if necessary.

managing high blood pressure

SIDE-EFFECTS ASSOCIATED WITH ANTIHYPERTENSIVES

Drug class	Possible side-effects
Thiazide/thiazide-like diuretics (e.g. Aprinox®)	• Low potassium levels in the blood (detected by blood tests). • Impaired glucose tolerance (higher than normal blood glucose levels) particularly when combined with a beta-blocker (detected by blood tests). • Raised LDL cholesterol, triglycerides and uric acid (detected by blood and urine tests). • Erectile dysfunction (male impotence). • Gout.
Alpha-blockers (e.g. Cardura®)	• Stress incontinence in women. • Dizziness on standing.
Beta-blockers (e.g. Cardicor®)	• Worsening of glucose control (detected by blood tests). • Lethargy. • Impaired concentration and memory, vivid dreams. • Erectile dysfunction (male impotence). • Worsening of the symptoms of peripheral arterial disease (or poor circulation to the legs). • Raynaud's disease (white 'bloodless' fingers and toes).
Dihydropyridine calcium-channel blockers (e.g. Amlostin®)	• Peripheral oedema (fluid accumulation and swelling in the ankles, for example). • Overgrowing gums. • Flushing and headaches.
Non-dihydropyridine calcium-channel blockers (e.g. Tildiem®)	• Reduced force and rate of heart beat. • Constipation.
ACE inhibitors (e.g. Capoten®)	• Persistent dry cough. • Poor kidney function. • Hypotension (acute, initial drops in blood pressure). • Angioedema (swelling beneath the skin, especially around the eyes and lips). • Occasional rash.
Angiotensin receptor blockers (e.g. Amias®)	• Dizziness. • Side-effects are rarely reported with this type of drug.

CERTAIN PATIENTS SHOULD AVOID CERTAIN ANTIHYPERTENSIVES

- Beta-blockers should not be used if you are asthmatic or have chronic obstructive pulmonary disease (COPD). Beta-blockers may also increase the likelihood of developing diabetes, particularly if they are used in combination with thiazide or thiazide-like diuretics.
- Certain calcium-channel blockers (e.g. verapamil and diltiazem) should not be used if you have heart failure. They should also be used with extreme caution in combination with beta-blockers.
- Thiazide or thiazide-like diuretics should be avoided if you have a history of gout or you are taking lithium.
- ACE inhibitors and angiotensin receptor blockers should not be used if you are pregnant. These drugs are also not generally used if you have kidney disease, although in some cases these can be prescribed and supervised by a specialist.

YOUR DOCTOR MAY PRESCRIBE YOU OTHER DRUGS

Aspirin

If you are at high risk for heart disease or stroke then your doctor may advise you to take aspirin (75 mg) every day. Aspirin thins your blood and makes it more difficult for your blood to clot. If you are sensitive to aspirin, you may be prescribed other drugs that have the same effects, such as clopidogrel (Plavix®).

Statins

Statins are recommended by the British Hypertension Society for anyone with cardiovascular disease or at a high risk of developing cardiovascular disease and also for people with diabetes.

Many studies have shown that taking statins on a regular basis can help to reduce the number of deaths from cardiovascular disease. In people who have already experienced angina, peripheral arterial disease, a heart attack or a stroke it is now commonplace to take both aspirin and a statin in addition to your antihypertensive medication. Your doctor will tell you if this is appropriate for you.

TREATING SPECIAL PATIENT GROUPS

Older people

In older people, blood pressure varies greatly between seated and standing positions and so it is important to measure blood pressure in a standing position and also to measure it on several occasions. It is estimated that more than half of the UK's population older than 60 have high blood pressure, and in the majority of cases this will be in the form of Isolated Systolic Hypertension (or ISH) where only the systolic blood pressure (the higher number) is raised. The dihydropyridine calcium-channel blockers (C) and the thiazide/thiazide-like diuretics (D) are particularly effective in older people. This is reflected in the ABCD rule shown previously where these two classes of drugs are considered to be the first choice of treatment in older people over 55.

Younger people

Most of the research and guidance for blood pressure management has been performed in people over the age of 30 and, in many cases, over the age of 50. This does not mean that young people do not get high blood pressure. A high diastolic blood pressure is more common in younger people than a high systolic blood pressure, whilst secondary hypertension (high blood pressure caused by a specific underlying condition) is more common in younger patients. The lifestyle changes described earlier have the same benefits whatever your age, and it is strongly

When treating hypertension in younger people, the doctor will first determine if there is an underlying reason for it.

recommended that these lifestyle changes are adopted at as early an age as possible for maximum benefit to your cardiovascular health. The benefits of exercise and a healthy diet in early life will certainly be rewarded as we grow older.

Ethnic groups

Clinical studies of large groups of people have shown that people of African or Afro-Caribbean origin have higher blood pressures than people who are Caucasian (white). Hypertension in people of African origin is generally more sensitive to salt in the diet, which is likely to be linked to the functioning of their renin–angiotensin systems. Black people generally have lower levels of renin.

Other ethnic groups that tend to have higher blood pressure are those of Mexican, Indian or Hawaiian origin. The South Asian population in particular appear to be prone to diabetes. This combination of factors leads to an increased risk for heart disease and stroke and makes an effective blood pressure management plan of paramount importance in these populations.

Thiazide diuretics and calcium-channel blockers (rather than beta-blockers, angiotensin receptor blockers or ACE inhibitors) appear to be the most effective form of drug treatment for this population of patients.

DIABETES

Having diabetes greatly increases your cardiovascular risk, even if your blood pressure is relatively normal. As a consequence of this increased risk, guidelines have created a lower blood pressure target for diabetic patients compared with the rest of the population.

The use of ACE inhibitors or angiotensin receptor blockers is a common first choice of therapy for people with diabetes. It is also common for a person with diabetes and hypertension to require at least three different types of blood pressure-lowering drug. This combination is likely to include a diuretic and an ACE inhibitor or an angiotensin receptor blocker. Calcium-channel blockers, beta-blockers and alpha-blockers may also be used in combination. Finally, since diabetes is such a strong predictor of heart disease and stroke, it is also usual to prescribe a statin to anyone who has both diabetes and hypertension.

The risk of vascular complications, and the risk of death, is doubled in people who have both hypertension and diabetes.

If you are diabetic and hypertensive you should aim to reduce your blood pressure to below 130/80 mmHg. People with diabetes are likely to be prescribed blood pressure-lowering drugs straight away.

managing high blood pressure

METABOLIC SYNDROME

The metabolic syndrome is a collection of conditions that increase your chance of developing heart disease, stroke and diabetes. To diagnose this syndrome your doctor will take a blood sample to test your blood fat and blood sugar levels, will measure your blood pressure and will also measure your waist. If you have any three of the following five factors you may be diagnosed as having the metabolic syndrome.

1. Abdominal obesity – a waist size over 102 cm (men) or over 88 cm (women).
2. High triglycerides – a type of 'bad fat' (above 1.7 mmol/L).
3. Low levels of high density lipoprotein (HDL) cholesterol – a type of 'good' cholesterol (0.9 mmol/L or lower in men and 1.1 mmol/L or lower in women).
4. High glucose (blood sugar) – an indicator of pre-diabetes (above 5.6 mmol/L).
5. Raised blood pressure above 130/85 mmHg.

The good news is that all of these characteristics can be tackled by a healthy diet and exercise, and where necessary drug treatment.

> The metabolic syndrome is really just a way of grouping people who are at high risk of heart disease.

KIDNEY DISEASE

Kidney disease is a common cause of secondary hypertension. The control of blood pressure and blockade of the renin–angiotensin system are two good ways of preserving kidney function. Thus, ACE inhibitors or angiotensin receptor blockers are a common first choice of antihypertensive therapy in people with evidence of kidney disease. The majority of people with kidney disease in addition to hypertension will require more than one type of antihypertensive therapy and a diuretic is a common additional choice of drug in these individuals.

STROKE

In people who have suffered a stroke, it is unclear whether antihypertensive treatment should be continued or stopped immediately after the stroke. However, usual practice is to restart therapy a couple of weeks after the event. It is also common to be prescribed aspirin and/or a statin in order to reduce the risk of future cardiovascular events like other strokes and heart attacks. Thiazide diuretics and/or ACE inhibitors are common choices of antihypertensive therapy in people who have suffered a stroke.

High blood pressure is the major preventable risk factor for stroke.

THE COMBINED ORAL CONTRACEPTIVE

The use of the combined oral contraceptive pill (e.g. Microgynon®) tends to increase blood pressure by an average of 5/3 mmHg. In a small proportion of women (~1%), severe hypertension may occur. Women taking the combined oral contraceptive pill should ensure that their blood pressure is checked every 6–12 months. Those women who are diagnosed with hypertension whilst on the combined oral contraceptive pill are generally switched to a progesterone-only contraceptive pill or an alternative method of contraception, which do not appear to be associated with increases in blood pressure.

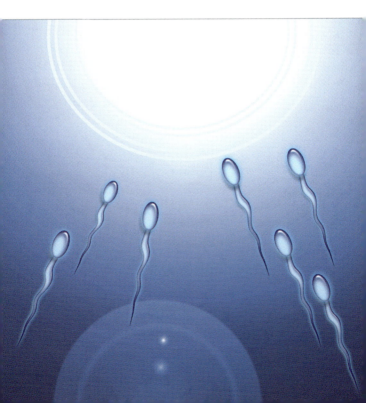

HIGH BLOOD PRESSURE DURING PREGNANCY

Pregnancy can be accompanied by a rise in the mother's blood pressure. In 1 in 10 pregnancies, mild pre-eclampsia occurs – this is defined as hypertension occurring after week 20 of the pregnancy and is usually accompanied by protein in the urine (proteinuria). Very rarely (about 1 in 3,500 women), and if left untreated, pre-eclampsia can progress to eclampsia which can potentially endanger the lives of the mother or their baby. In the majority of cases, a slightly raised blood pressure is just another facet of your pregnancy and is no significant cause for concern.

Women with pre-existing essential hypertension and pre-eclampsia are also at an increased risk of intrauterine growth retardation (this means that the foetus is smaller than expected).

As we have seen, ACE inhibitors and angiotensin receptor blockers are not suitable for you during pregnancy, or if you are trying to become pregnant, since they may cause harm to the unborn baby during the latter stages of pregnancy. Your doctor will prescribe an alternative blood pressure-lowering drug that is not associated with any undesirable side-effects for either the mother or the baby.

Hypertension occurs in 8–10% of all pregnancies.

ALTERNATIVE TREATMENTS

There is increasing interest amongst patients in the use of alternative medicines for the treatment of all kinds of ailments and disorders. This includes natural remedies like herbs, supplements and extracts, together with physical techniques such as meditation or acupuncture. The difficulty that the scientific community and government bodies face with regard to advising us on these approaches to healthcare is that evidence of their effectiveness is largely anecdotal. Some of the more commonly used remedies and techniques have been subjected to more scientific trials, but these have generally been conducted in very small numbers of people (less than 100) whereas trials of conventional drugs are generally conducted in hundreds or thousands of people.

Natural remedies are not licensed by the same regulatory authorities that control the use of medicines, and so their content cannot be guaranteed to be pure or safe. In contrast, prescription drugs in the UK are licensed and regulated by the Medicines and Healthcare Products Regulatory Agency (MHRA). This agency ensures that all medicines sold in the UK for human use are of acceptable standard, quality and efficacy.

It is important to inform and consult with your doctor before embarking on any form of natural, alternative or complementary medicine.

a simple guide to blood pressure

NON-HERBAL THERAPIES WITH SOME EVIDENCE OF BLOOD PRESSURE-LOWERING EFFECTS

Transcendental meditation	A type of meditation believed to reduce blood pressure by relieving the symptoms of stress.
Yoga	Yoga reduces anxiety, promotes well-being, and can improve your quality of life in general.
Ayurveda	A program of herbal preparations, diet, yoga, meditation and other practices, which focuses on the body, mind and consciousness. Some components of the Ayurvedic treatment may lower blood pressure.
Acupuncture	Very fine needles are inserted into the skin at specific anatomic points to stimulate and balance the movement of energy (Chi) in the body. Acupuncture can have beneficial effects on the immune system and the circulation.
Chi gong	A traditional Chinese exercise consisting of breathing and gentle movements.

HERBAL REMEDIES OR NATURAL THERAPIES WITH SOME EVIDENCE OF BLOOD PRESSURE-LOWERING EFFECTS

Coenzyme Q10	Within the body this chemical helps cells to create energy from nutrients. Coenzyme Q10 supplements have been shown to reduce blood pressure and blood cholesterol levels. The most effective dose appears to be around 225 mg per day.
Garlic (*Allium sativum*)	Garlic can help to thin your blood and stop it from clogging up your arteries in much the same way as aspirin does. Several clinical studies have shown that dried garlic preparations (of 600–900 mg/day) can help to lower blood pressure if taken over several months.

Other vitamins, extracts, and herbal remedies for which there is some evidence for antihypertensive properties include:

- vitamins E and C
- L-Arginine
- hawthorn extract
- grape juice
- pomegranate juice
- ginseng root
- taurine
- arjuna bark
- olive leaf
- European mistletoe
- yarrow
- black cumin seeds
- forskolin
- Indian snakeroot.

NATURAL REMEDIES TO AVOID IF YOU HAVE HIGH BLOOD PRESSURE

Liquorice (*Glycyrrhiza glabra*)	This herb (the dried root or root extract) can raise your blood pressure and has the potential to result in heart failure. It should not be used if you have liver, kidney or cardiovascular disorders, if you are pregnant, have low blood potassium or are hypertensive.
Ma Huang (*Ephedra sinica*)	This herb should not be used if you have hypertension, diabetes, thyroid disease or a heart condition.
Asian ginseng (*Panax ginseng*)	There are some reports that certain types of ginseng may cause high blood pressure as a side-effect.

THE LONG AND THE SHORT OF IT

Is high blood pressure life-threatening?

Since you generally won't feel any symptoms from having a raised blood pressure it is easy to ignore it and hard to imagine that it is doing you any harm. However, high blood pressure is called 'the silent killer' for a reason and, as scary as it sounds, if you leave it untreated then you are putting yourself at a greater risk of developing heart or kidney disease, or suffering a stroke later in life. Together, heart disease and stroke remain the biggest killers in the UK today. The good news is that high blood pressure can be managed and controlled effectively. Adopting lifestyle changes and/or taking appropriate drug therapy can dramatically reduce your blood pressure and hugely reduce your risk of life-threatening events.

Will it go away on its own?

High blood pressure won't go away on its own. In fact, as you get older your blood pressure has a natural tendency to rise. If you have a healthy diet rich in fresh produce, low in salt and low in saturated fats, and you remain fit and active, then you are well on the way to keeping your blood pressure at a healthy level and reducing your risk of cardiovascular disease. But even fit and healthy people can suffer from high blood pressure. Therefore, it is vital that you have your blood pressure checked regularly and that you take any drugs your doctor prescribes regularly.

managing high blood pressure

GETTING THE MOST OUT OF YOUR HEALTH SERVICE

It is important that you maintain a good relationship with your doctor or nurse in order that your blood pressure is controlled effectively. This includes making your best efforts to follow the treatment plan that you and your doctor or nurse come up with. It also means ensuring that you make regular appointments with your doctor or nurse to monitor how your blood pressure is changing over time and with treatment. You may also wish to keep a record of your blood pressure readings yourself. If you would like to monitor your blood pressure at home then it is a good idea to discuss this with your doctor or nurse.

Every patient is different and it is very common for your doctor to change the antihypertensive drugs you are prescribed in order to provide the best possible control of your blood pressure with the minimum of side-effects. You may find that your local doctor's surgery has a clinic which deals specifically with cardiovascular issues such as helping you to improve your diet or quit smoking, and will regularly measure your blood pressure too. These are likely to be run by nurses, occasionally with the help of dietitians and pharmacists, and are a fantastic way of helping you to tackle your high blood pressure.

If you experience any side-effects of a new drug then tell your doctor immediately – there are many other antihypertensive drugs you can take.

If you are prescribed a blood pressure-lowering drug then don't be surprised if you are prescribed two or even three different drugs – this is perfectly normal and is actually recommended by the British Hypertension Society. Most people with hypertension will probably need to take more than one drug.

Lifestyle measures can lower your blood pressure just as effectively as antihypertensive drugs. These changes are best regarded as changes for life rather than a temporary means of reducing your blood pressure. A combination of lifestyle change and drug therapy is usually the best way to restore your blood pressure to healthy levels.

Once your blood pressure is reduced to its optimal level you will usually need to continue with your management plan indefinitely in order to keep your blood pressure low. Your doctor will advise you for how long you should continue to take any medication.

QUESTIONS TO ASK YOUR DOCTOR

- Exactly how high is my blood pressure?
- What should my blood pressure be?
- How low should I expect it to get if I follow my treatment plan?
- For how long should I take this medication?
- How often should I come back and get my blood pressure checked?
- How often should I come back to get my blood cholesterol checked?
- Will this medicine interact with any other medicines I am on?
- Are there any side-effects associated with this medicine?
- What kind of lifestyle changes should I be making?
- Is my blood pressure dangerously high or only slightly high?
- What will happen to me if I don't take this medication?

simple extras

FURTHER READING

- *BESTMEDICINE Hypertension* (2005)
  320pp, ISBN 1-905064-99-3 £13.95

- **Guidelines for management of hypertension**: Report of the fourth working party of the British Hypertension Society (BHS IV). Williams B, Poulter NR, Brown MJ *et al. J Hum Hypertension* 2004; **18**: 139–185.

- **PRODIGY guidance – Hypertension (April 2003)**
  London: Department of Health.
  www.prodigy.nhs.uk/guidance.asp?gt=Hypertension

USEFUL CONTACTS

- **Action on Smoking and Health**
  Tel: 020 7739 5902
  Website: *www.ash.org.uk*

- **Blood Pressure Association**
  60 Cranmer Terrace
  London
  SW17 0QS
  Tel: 020 8772 4994
  Website: *www.bpassoc.org.uk/index.htm*

- **British Acupuncture Council**
  Park House
  206–208 Latimer Road
  London
  W10 6RE
  Tel: 020 8735 0400
  Website: *www.acupuncture.org.uk*

- **British Heart Foundation**
  14 Fitzhardinge Street
  London
  W1H 6DH
  Tel: 020 7935 0185
  Website: *www.bhf.org.uk*
  Heart information line: 08450 70 80 70

- **British Hypertension Society**
  BHS Information Service
  Blood Pressure Unit
  St George's Hospital Medical School
  Cranmer Terrace
  London
  SW17 0RE
  Tel: 020 8725 3412
  Email: *bhsis@sghms.ac.uk*
  Website: *www.bhsoc.org*

- **British Nutrition Foundation**
  High Holborn House
  52–54 High Holborn
  London
  WC1V 6RQ
  Tel: 020 7404 6504
  Email: *postbox@nutrition.org.uk*
  Website: *www.nutrition.org.uk*

- **British Wheel of Yoga**
  BWY Central Office
  25 Jermyn Street
  Sleaford
  NG34 7RU
  Tel: 01529 306851
  Website: *www.bwy.org.uk*
  Email: *office@bwy.org.uk*

- **Heart UK**
  7 North Road
  Maidenhead
  SL6 1PE
  Tel: 01628 628638
  Website: *www.heartuk.org.uk*
  Email: *ask@heartuk.org.uk*

- **High Blood Pressure Foundation**
  Department of Medical Sciences
  Western General Hospital
  Edinburgh
  EH4 2XU
  Tel: 0131 332 9211
  Website: *www.hbpf.org.uk*
  Email: *hbpf@hbpf.org.uk*

- **Kidney Patient Guide website**
  www.kidneypatientguide.org.uk/site/contents.php

- **National Heart Forum**
  Tavistock House South
  Tavistock Square
  London
  WC1H 9LG
  Tel: 020 7383 7638
  Website: *www.heartforum.org.uk*
  Email: *webenquiry@heartforum.org.uk*

- **NHS Smoking Adviceline**
  Tel: 0800 1690169

■ **The Patients Association**
PO Box 935
Harrow
Middlesex
HA1 3XJ
Helpline: 0845 608 4455
Tel: 020 8423 9111
Website: *www.patients-association.com*

■ **The Stroke Association**
240 City Road
London
EC1V 2PR
Tel: 020 7566 0300
Website: *www.stroke.org.uk*
Email: *info@stroke.org.uk*
National Stroke Helpline: 0845 30 33 100

■ **Weightwatchers**
3rd Floor North Wing
Hines Meadow
St Cloud Way
Maidenhead
SL6 8XB
Email: *uk.help@weightwatchers.co.uk*
Website: *www.weightwatchers.co.uk*

YOUR RIGHTS

As a patient, you have a number of important rights. These include the right to the best possible standard of care, the right to information, the right to dignity and respect, the right to confidentiality and underpinning all of these, the right to good health.

Occasionally, you may feel as though your rights have been compromised, or you may be unsure of where you stand when it comes to qualifying for certain treatments or services. In these instances, there are a number of organisations you can turn to for help and advice. Remember that lodging a complaint against your health service should not compromise the quality of care you receive, either now or in the future.

- **Patients Association**
  The Patients Association (*www.patients-association.com*) is a UK charity which represents patient rights, influences health policy and campaigns for better patient care.
  Contact details:
  PO Box 935
  Harrow
  Middlesex
  HA1 3YJ
  Helpline: 08456 084455
  Email: *mailbox@patients-association.com*

- **Citizens Advice Bureau**
  The Citizens Advice Bureau (*www.nacab.org.uk*) provides free, independent and confidential advice to NHS patients at a number of outreach centres located throughout the country (*www.adviceguide.org.uk*).
  Contact details:
  Find your local Citizens Advice Bureau using the search tool at *www.citizensadvice.org.uk*

■ **Patient Advice and Liaison Services (PALS)**
Set up by the Department of Health (*www.dh.gov.uk*), PALS provide information, support and confidential advice to patients, families and their carers.
Contact details:
Phoning your local hospital, clinic, GP surgery or health centre and ask for details of the PALS, or call NHS Direct on 0845 46 47.

■ **The Independent Complaints Advocacy Service (ICAS)**
ICAS is an independent service that can help you bring about formal complaints against your NHS practitioner. ICAS provides support, help, advice and advocacy from experienced advisors and caseworkers.
Contact details:
ICAS Central Team
Myddelton House
115–123 Pentonville Road
London N1 9LZ
Email: *icascentralteam@citizensadvice.org.uk*
Or contact your local ICAS office direct.

Accessing your medical records

You have a legal right to see all your health records under the Data Protection Act of 1998. You can usually make an informal request to your doctor and you should be given access within 40 days. Note that you may have to pay a small fee for the privilege.

You can be denied access to your records if your doctor believes that the information contained within them could cause serious harm to you or another person. If you are applying for access on behalf of someone else, then you will not be granted access to information which the patient gave to his or her doctor on the understanding that it would remain confidential.

PERSONAL RECORD:

My Simple Guide

This Simple Guide to Blood Pressure belongs to:

Name:

Address:

Tel No:

Email:

In case of emergency please contact:

Name:

Address:

Tel No:

Email:

simple extras

My Healthcare Team

GP surgery address and telephone number

Name:

Address:

Tel No:

I am registered with Dr

My practice nurse

My hospital specialist

My pharmacist

Other members of my healthcare team

QUESTIONS

ANSWERS

a simple guide to blood pressure

NOTES